Cambridge Elements ≡

Elements in Public Policy

edited by
M. Ramesh
National University of Singapore
Michael Howlett
Simon Fraser University, British Columbia
Xun Wu
Hong Kong University of Science and Technology
Judith Clifton
University of Cantabria
Eduardo Araral
National University of Singapore

MAKING GLOBAL POLICY

Diane Stone
Central European University

CAMBRIDGE
UNIVERSITY PRESS

University Printing House, Cambridge CB2 8BS, United Kingdom

One Liberty Plaza, 20th Floor, New York, NY 10006, USA

477 Williamstown Road, Port Melbourne, VIC 3207, Australia

314–321, 3rd Floor, Plot 3, Splendor Forum, Jasola District Centre,
New Delhi – 110025, India

79 Anson Road, #06–04/06, Singapore 079906

Cambridge University Press is part of the University of Cambridge.

It furthers the University's mission by disseminating knowledge in the pursuit of
education, learning, and research at the highest international levels of excellence.

www.cambridge.org
Information on this title: www.cambridge.org/9781108724753
DOI: 10.1017/9781108661690

First published 2020

A catalogue record for this publication is available from the British Library.

ISBN 978-1-108-72475-3 Paperback
ISSN 2398-4058 (online)
ISSN 2514-3565 (print)

Making Global Policy

Elements in Public Policy

DOI: 10.1017/9781108661690
First published online: November 2019

Diane Stone
Central European University
Author for correspondence: Diane Stone Stone@ceu.edu

Abstract: Global policy making is taking shape in a wide range of public-sector activities managed by transnational policy communities. Public policy scholars have long recognised the impact of globalisation on the industrialised knowledge economies of OECD states, as well as on social and economic policy challenges faced by developing and transition states. But the focus has been on domestic politics and policy. Today, the Policy Studies literature is building new concepts of 'transnational public–private partnership', 'trans-governmentalism' and 'science diplomacy' to account for rapid growth of global policy networks and informal international organisations delivering public goods and services. This Element goes beyond traditional texts which focus on public policy as an activity of states to outline how global policy making has driven many global and regional transformations over the past quarter century.

This title is also available as Open Access on Cambridge Core at doi.org /10.1017/9781108661690.

Keywords: evidence-based policy; global policy; policy network; public sphere; science diplomacy; transnational public–private partnership

Isbns: 9781108724753 (PB), 9781108661690 (OC)
Issns: 2398-4058 (online), 2514-3565 (print)

Contents

1 Public Policy for Global Problems   1

2 Creating Global Policy: Public and Private Constructions   6

3 Transnational Networks: Policy in Partnership   27

4 Global Policy Persuasion: From Evidence-Based Policy to
   Science Diplomacy   47

5 Navigating Global Policy Processes   65

   List of Abbreviations   71

   References   74

1 Public Policy for Global Problems

Global problems are everywhere. So too are many answers to these problems. But our capacity to create global public policies to deal with these problems seems to be a case of too little, too late. Oftentimes the causes of problems are already well known. Communities of scientists, researchers and other kinds of 'experts' who might be based in a university, independent scientific body or government agency have provided a wealth of theories, data or other forms of evidence with some kind of scientifically rigorous explanation or analysis of problems. Many times, these experts and scientists are pressed into being advisers, to explain to government or society at large what the problem is and what causes the problem as well as to provide solutions. Yet, problems persist and are particularly 'wicked': global problems grow at a faster rate than the mustering of inter-state cooperation to deal with them.

Global policy problems are 'wicked' because they are very difficult, sometimes impossible, to solve for many reasons: first, incomplete or contradictory knowledge creating uncertainty; second, the number of countries, communities and other interests involved with quite disparate values; third, the multiple arenas for deliberation; and fourth, the interconnected nature of many global issues with other problems (Geuijen et al., 2017; Head, 2013). International policy coordination to deliver collective action and implement a set of genuine global responses is often slow and incomplete, while effectiveness is often riven by non-compliance.

Global problems are multifarious. Take disease, for example. Disease does not respect national borders; it travels in the bilge water of tankers traversing international sea lanes, spreading waterborne disease like cholera (Lee, 2001). Disease travels in business class with sick passengers on a plane (Budd et al., 2009). The worldwide rise of some non-communicable diseases in our societies may have resulted as one of the many perversities of industrialised food production, with high fat, sugar or preservative content contributing to diabetes and obesity (Heasman and Lang, 2015). Today, there is a scientific consensus that smoking tobacco contributes to higher worldwide incidence of certain cancers – a concern which led to the Framework Convention on Tobacco Control (FCTC) (Mamudu et al., 2015).

Human lives, from cradle to grave, are touched by global and regional dynamics. This touch is unevenly spread and has dramatically different outcomes across states and societies. Regardless, global policy problems affect us all in some way. This is also felt in everyday life through the transnational regulations, 'soft laws' or global rankings and targets that shape policy, particularly in areas like the seventeen goals of the SDGs – the Sustainable

Development Goals led by the United Nations (UN), which came into effect from 2016. National deference to 'international best practice' or the policy pronouncements and procedures of leading transnational actors in global governance also tie the fate of one country or community to those of others elsewhere in the world. In this milieu, various types of experts, policy consultants and scientific advisers seek not only to provide evidence to support global policy development but also to consolidate their power in global policy making.

Epistocracies may well be emerging. The concept of epistocracy is usually associated with giving more educated and expert constituents greater voting power, or even limiting votes only to the educated. This conflates the concept with electoral contests. *Epistocracy* has wider meaning as 'knowledge-based rule' or 'rule by knowers' (Klocksiem, 2019). It is a form of power that entails giving the more educated or expert actors greater judgement in decision-making processes (Holst, 2012; Reiss, 2019). Epistocracy is a useful concept to capture knowledge-based decision-making as well as knowledge networking between states and in transnational policy communities.

Global policy incorporates both governmentally steered processes of 'international public policy', better known today as 'trans-governmentalism', and 'transnational policy processes' where there is a greater degree of authoritative steering from non-state actors. The word *transnational* will be encountered far more frequently in this Element than the words *international* or *intergovernmental*. The latter two words speak to formal political relations between nation-states. By contrast, *transnational* recognises the integral roles of business, civil society and scientific actors in global and regional policy making. Recognising these distinctions draws attention to a new sub-field of Policy Studies, that is, 'global policy' studies. In tandem, this Element also develops the new policy concept of 'epistocracy' as one power dynamic behind global policy making.

Policy making that supersedes the nation-state is undergoing three interconnected revolutions. First, policy making is witnessing a diversification of the goals it is expected to pursue by going beyond traditional objectives of supporting national communities and local economies. Policy making is now adjoined to additional tasks of financing, or otherwise supporting and delivering 'global public goods' (GPGs) (Kaul, 2019). Second, new domains of public action above and beyond the nation-state – in part created by rapid advances in information technology that have eased the flow of communication alongside far faster and cheaper means of travel – have prompted an increase in the number and diversity of policy actors. Official actors – governments and international organisations – have become partners in global policy with private actors in the corporate world and civil society. Third, the instruments used by this expanding array of actors to achieve a broader range of policy objectives have themselves mushroomed with the emergence of transnational policy institutions, innovative regulatory structures and global networks created to deliver, finance or monitor regional and global GPGs. These circumstances also generate a governance conundrum by fuelling the fragmentation of global policy into many different 'sectors', a dynamic also known as 'differentiation' (Sending, 2019).

In this changing context of global policy making, science is often said to be 'universal'. This commonplace saying is meant to convey the idea that science has the features of a public good. That is, knowledge – in the form of human understanding, or data sets and theories – has the capacity, or contains the seeds of innovation, for resolving pressing social and economic concerns. The processes that underpin global science – funding regimes, international knowledge exchange, peer review and publication and academic conferences – are also increasingly globalised. This is seen in international scholarship schemes, in associations like the Global Research Council or the International Network for Government Science Advice (INGSA) and in the emergence of international branch campuses or joint research programmes of universities. Those working in the multifaceted world of science and scholarship are often tasked to provide evidence and help find solutions to alleviate or remedy the range of global problems that seem to be proliferating.

By introducing the new concept of 'global policy', the objective of this Element is threefold: first, to draw attention to the burgeoning literature on global policy; second, to outline some of the network innovations and policy partnerships for delivering global policies; and third, to look at how experts, scientists and other knowledge actors participate in global policy processes. As policy instruments of global governance, policy networks and partnerships do not exercise the same degree of authority that government exercises. Instead, this Element argues that they tend to be reliant more so on the epistemic authority that comes from the evidence created by experts. Through practices such as science diplomacy, epistocracy is a form of power that may consolidate in global policy making. Yet, state sovereignty continues to be an important rein upon the authority of new transnational actors. The state is not in retreat. There are many opportunities for states to reconfigure their roles and responsibilities in global policy processes.

The next section introduces the reader to global policy processes and various endeavours to develop a common 'conceptual grammar'. The discussion provides a snapshot of 'global policy studies' and addresses the overlapping fields of Global Governance and Policy Studies. A long-standing scholarly link between the two fields of inquiry is 'public goods' theory. Another concept from Policy Studies that has also been used to interpret global governance dynamics is the 'policy community' idea (Broome and Seabrooke, 2015).

Transnational policy communities are composed of actors from government agencies and international organisations as well as other relevant 'stakeholders' from the professions, academia, business and civil society, including leading non-governmental organisations (NGOs) and international philanthropies. They coalesce around specific policy issues and are 'networked across globally distributed sites of knowledge production and exchange' (Prince, 2010). These communities often seek to build and entrench a policy paradigm – a consensual way of thinking about and acting upon specific policy problems – which specifies both a set of instruments and a set of goals to be pursued using these instruments (Babb, 2013: 272). In many instances, transnational policy communities have become social ecologies and cultural epistocracies 'where respect for knowledge and knowers is considerable and many subscribe to the idea that decision-making must be knowledge-based and knowers must play a significant role in decision-making' (Holst, 2012: 4). This is a broad notion of decision-making that includes problem definition and agenda setting as well as many decisions made in the course of the operationalisation and review of policy.

Transnational policy communities are treated here as manifestations of a distinctly *global* public sector. Organisational actors and their networks in these communities engage in global policy making, public financing and service delivery around policy issue areas or specific problems. But unlike national public sectors organised under the hierarchical control of the state, the global public sector is much more decentralised (from singular sovereign control), devolved (to many private-sector and civil society bodies) and disaggregated (across scales of governance). The *global* public sector emerges partly from a delegation by states of administrative powers and functions but also, if not more so, from the gradual accrual of responsibilities, funds and mandates by these communities, which operate with their own professional interests and policy coordination ambitions.

Section 3 outlines the diversity of network structure and composition. For instance, trans-governmental networks are composed entirely of government officials. By contrast, public–private partnerships bring in private-sector actors to help tackle global problems. These and other types of networks are global policy instruments. In many instances, the inclusion of corporate-sector and civil society interests as 'stakeholders' in the management of global policy problems provides some legitimacy for the network. As sovereign authority is often lacking in global policy making, transnational policy communities also seek legitimation through expert knowledge and a (social) scientific consensus the community can use for legitimation and to bolster their policy paradigm.

The fourth section focuses on the transnational actors and policy communities involved in evidence-based policy making for global governance. One manifestation of evidence-based policy is science diplomacy. This is the 'persuasion' component of global policy making: scientific input to policy making – in the form of data, models or analysis – has become increasingly contested in an era of 'alternative facts' (EL-CSID, 2019). Nevertheless, scientific consensus and policy advice remain important foundations that give direction to cooperative action and policy development. Epistemic authority is one important pillar upon which policy paradigms are built. However, this Element ends on the note that science, evidence and the 'facts' do not provide all the answers. Just as is the case at the city level of governance, global policy making is not simply a normative endeavour to create 'a better world' but is also shaped by the practices of the powerful. 'Epistocracy' concentrates political power among those with superior knowledge of the complexity of public problems and policy processes. In the absence of a global citizenry with rights and responsibilities, the democratic void in most transnational policy spaces potentially provides fertile ground for rule by experts or other powerful interests.

Yet, the impetus towards global policy making, and the rise of transnational policy communities, is not inevitable. The political will and 'appetite' for international collaboration and multilateralism that was evident at the turn of the millennium is today in short supply. In the wake of the 2008 global financial crisis, and the populist-nationalist politics and policies of leaders such as Bolsonaro in Brazil, Órban in Hungary, Duterte in the Philippines and Trump in the USA, the 'appetite' for 'global policies' has abated. Instead, global policy is often dismissed and denigrated as being designed by those portrayed as unaccountable transnational elites who are disconnected from national communities. Even so, global problems persist and proliferate. While collective action and policy responses to these problems are deficient, this makes it all the more pressing to better conceptualise 'global policy'.

Making Global Policy takes one of the great strengths of public policy as a *field* of study – that is, its multidisciplinary character – to draw upon theories and concepts developed in economics, international political economy, law, political geography, political science and social policy. However, the analysis in the subsequent sections goes beyond the 'methodological nationalism' of traditional Policy Studies texts which focus on 'public policy' as an activity controlled by states, inside states or between states. The intention is to 'scale up' Policy Studies in light of the global governance transformations that have taken place over the past quarter century. Everyday understanding of the extent and substance of what is legitimate rule – the norms, practices and mechanisms guiding and structuring public life – often runs on a political philosophy that peaked from the end of the nineteenth century to the late twentieth century. In a nutshell, our categories, concepts and theories do not necessarily fit anymore with political realities and the policy ills that appear increasingly concurrent with the rising complexity of cross-national economic life and transnational sociocultural engagements. The proliferation of transnational policy networks is symptomatic. But these networks and the partnership 'instruments' they build are not just global policy *tools*; they are also constellations of administrative actors that give life to transnational policy communities. In other words, networks can be seen as both structures and agents.

The maturing of global policy programmes signals innovations in transnational administrative praxis in an era that is witness to rapid reconfigurations of sovereignty. A conceptual ambition in this Elements is to develop and distinguish between the inter-related ideas of 'trans-governmentalism', 'transnational administration' and 'science diplomacy'. For these ideas to have traction requires a move away from the 'methodological nationalism' of Policy Studies to address the new spaces of authoritative public action and policy making that are not centred solely around nation-states. Instead, new policy-making spaces emerge through global and regional partnerships and networks. These spaces are occupied by multiple actors engaged in financing, delivering or managing GPGs. Once these spaces are recognised as 'public sectors', it is possible to develop an appreciation of 'methodological transnationalism'.

Finally, this Elements can only touch upon some normative concerns and dilemmas of transparency, representation and accountability of transnational policy communities. These communities wield considerable decision-making powers in their policy domains but can become detached from the oversight mechanisms of traditional government authorities and national structures of democratic accountability or professional oversight. While epistocratic policy power is not necessarily at odds with democratically informed policy (Jeffrey, 2018), this kind of power is yet to be made fully compatible with democratic policy processes.

2 Creating Global Policy: Public and Private Constructions

'Whatever *governments* choose to do or not to do' is an oft-quoted definition of 'public policy' to be found in a popular textbook (Dye, 1984: 2, my emphasis). Another text defines policy as 'a statement by government – at whatever level, in whatever form – of what it intends to do about a public problem' (Birkland, 2016: 9). The Merriam-Webster (2019) online dictionary defines public policy as 'government policies that affect the whole population'. Many other sources and writers make similar definitions by putting government at the centre of policy making. This is understandable. Government is at the core of a nation-state's architecture. 'The state' is recognised as the sovereign power in international affairs. 'The state' is the highest authority in national policy. For the most part, policy scholars have reflected and reinforced this reality by treating the state as the core unit of analysis.

One objective here is to de-centre the state in emerging processes of global policy making. But this does not mean displacing the state or its authority. De-centring means, firstly, to identify and include private sources of policy making and delivery as equal partners to state actors regardless of whether these actors come from the market place or civil society. Secondly, de-centring entails recognising how state sovereignty has been transformed by globalisation with implications for public administration and policy making at national and sub-national levels. These pressures have brought new practices not only within the traditional policy setting of the nation-state but has also provoked new modalities of administration and policy coordination outside the nation-state.

Putting the state at the centre of analysis is known as 'methodological nationalism'. This section provides a brief review of the methodological nationalism of mainstream Policy Studies as a necessary precursor to introducing the concept of *methodological transnationalism*. The concept of methodological transnationalism helps us understand and map new forms of public-sector activity and transnational administration. The 'internationalisation' of public policy – such as occurs through policy transfer of instruments, tools or legislation across countries (inter alia Evans, 2019; Hadjiisky et al., 2017) or through official 'trans-governmental' policy coordination (Keohane and Nye, 1974; Legrand, 2015) – are relatively well advanced. These are processes where state actors continue to play a central role. Yet these two concepts are distinct from the ideas of 'transnational administration' or 'transnational policy communities' in which actors from the private sector or civil society play key roles in governance.

A second objective is to draw out the distinctiveness of a Policy Studies approach to global governance. This pursuit is not dissimilar to how legal scholars have developed the field of 'global administrative law' or GAL as it is known (Khoo, 2019; Machacek, 2018). The GAL school characterises global governance as administrative action which is also regulated by administrative principles, regulations and mechanisms with a law-like character, especially those relating to participation, transparency, accountability and review. A new generation of scholars in Global Policy Studies are developing their own arsenal of key concepts. This includes advancing notions such as the 'global public sphere'. It also includes applying the economic theory of public goods to analyse transnational policy problems and advocate for the provision of GPGs.

And some are now applying traditional policy concepts and theories to global policy phenomena. For example, the ideas of policy entrepreneur (Alimi, 2015) and 'public value' (Geuijin et al., 2017), or policy design principles (Peters et al., 2018). This disciplinary diversity helps keep the understandings of global governance in constant evolution.

Global Policy Studies: State of the Art

Policy scholarship has long addressed the impact of extra-state dynamics upon domestic politics (inter alia Farazmand and Pikowski, 2007; Reinicke, 1998; Skogstad, 2011; Soroos, 1986). Mainstream policy and public administration studies have also undertaken analysis of the capacity of public-sector hierarchies to globalise their national policies through cross-national learning and policy transfer (Hadjiisky et al., 2017). In tandem with the widening mandates and policy ambitions of international organisations over the past few decades, and the coalitions they form with governments or private-sector actors – such as companies, philanthropic foundations and other elements of civil society – a niche for Global Policy Studies has emerged (see Moloney and Stone, 2019).

A number of academic journals in the Policy Studies domain have already moved into in this niche. Journals such as *Global Governance, Global Policy, Global Summitry* and *Regulation and Governance* have been at the forefront of academic debate. *Public Administration* published a special issue on 'Global Public Policy and Transnational Administration' in 2015 and more articles since. There are also a few landmark books. The earliest was an edited collection *Global Policy Studies* (Nagel, 1991). However, the take-off in academic interest really occurred at the turn of the millennium sparked by books such as *Global Public Policy* (Reinicke, 1998) then later *Global Social Policy* (Deacon, 2007; Yeates, 2008) as well as *Global Public Policy: Business and the Countervailing Powers of Civil Society* (Ronit, 2007). A tipping point for the establishment of 'global policy studies' was reached with the publication of two *Handbooks* on the topic (Klassen et al., 2016; Stone and Moloney, 2019).

More frequently seen are academic studies that take a sector-specific focus. There are a plethora of studies of global health policy (see Šehović, 2017, for an overview). Likewise, the now extensive study of global environmental policy (or climate policy) is particularly noticeable (Biermann, 2009) as is scholarly work on overseas development assistance as a driver of global policy (Severino and Ray, 2009). Other smaller but significant bodies of research concern global refugee policy (e.g. Bauman and Miller, 2012) or global education policy (e.g. Green, 2016; Verger et al., 2012).

These sector-specific studies are indicative of the fragmentation of the study of global policy as an analytic endeavour. Three decades of scholarship has really only produced a handful of book-length studies focused directly on the concept of 'global (or transnational) policy' and global policy studies remains a specialised interest. One reason suggested for the sporadic nature of literature on global public policy is that it 'is commonly nested within other disciplines and issue-areas, rather than being a subject of scholarly inquiry in and of itself' (Bauman and Miller, 2012: 4; also Kaul, 2019: 270).

As a consequence, definitions of 'global (public) policy' are still evolving. For everyday people as well politicians and policy makers, the thought of public policy that is 'global' or 'transnational' remains unfamiliar and discomforting with 'big brother' overtones of 'world government'. 'Strictly speaking, there is no transnational state holding a global monopoly on the legitimate use of violence or other defining state features' (Ougaard, 2018: 130). Instead, 'the state' can be considered 'an umbrella concept that covers state *functions*, state *power* and state *apparatuses*'. Accordingly, it is possible to refer to the 'transnational state' as 'the unevenly and partially globalized aspects of statehood' (Ougaard, 2018: 130) that are driven by political, juridical and regulatory networks.

Sovereignty and the Westphalian Grammar

Respect for the principle of 'sovereignty' has been at the heart of Policy Studies and Public Administration. Sovereignty is a concept that has been extensively debated by International Relations (IR) scholars (Fanoulis and Musliu, 2018). The political philosopher Nancy Fraser has noted that this 'Westphalian political imaginary' maintains a sharp distinction between domestic and international space (Fraser, 2013: 181; Volkmer, 2019). Consequently, the literature on 'global policy', 'international public management' or 'transnational public administration' (or other cognate terms of analysis) is relatively sparse. With disciplinary boundaries firmly in place, the Policy Studies and Public Administration scholarly communities have sometimes missed opportunities to bring a distinct set of key concepts and analytical tools and theories of the policy process to the study of global governance.

Much ink has been spilt on the idea of 'sovereignty', and only a few ideas are addressed here. 'Westphalian sovereignty' is based on the principle that one sovereign state should not interfere in the domestic arrangements of another; that is, a state has legal immunity from external influences. By contrast, the notion of 'interdependence sovereignty' refers to the capacity and willingness of public authorities to control or regulate flows of people, goods and capital in and out of a country. 'Domestic sovereignty' is the capacity of a state to choose and implement policies within its territory (Krasner, 1999). The study of public policy often revolves around the latter two meanings (Stone and Ladi, 2015). These ideas are state-centric, where sovereignty is a property of a state. These ideas are also government-centric, where sovereignty is a territorial definition of political authority. Contemporary developments like the emergence of the European Union (EU) – where member states and EU institutions appear to be co-sovereigns – as well as the impact of some non-state actors on international organisations do qualify the notion of the complete supremacy of the state (Fanoulis and Musliu, 2018: 75). Theoretical developments such as the idea of a 'global public sphere' or of 'transnational administration' do so too.

The idea of 'administrative sovereignty' loosens the assumption of territorial or treaty boundaries defining sovereignty to focus on sovereignty as a set of practices and capabilities. In other words, 'administrative sovereignty is a function that a state, state-like, multiple-state or other actor can maintain with a reasonable measure of autonomy, credibility, and reliability over time' (Muth, 2019: 62). In this understanding, sovereignty is a spectrum of capacities; that is, the ability to initiate and implement. Transnational actors with administrative sovereignty could include private bodies like the credit rating agencies and other types of 'reputational intermediaries' such as international accreditation bodies in the higher education sector (Verger et al., 2012) or various professional organisations (Seabrooke and Henriksen, 2017). Rather than a static concept bound to the unitary state, 'everyday practices of sovereignty' – such as those generated by policy networks discussed in the next section – create new modes of public diplomacy and policy coordination that challenge but do not dispense with state driven modes of sovereignty (Fanoulis and Musliu, 2018: 72–5).

Fact and Fiction in Making Global Policy

'Global public policy' can be characterised as both a 'fact' and 'fiction'. It is a fiction in the sense that the continuing power of the sovereign state is not in doubt, although the state is being re-configured by global forces. But from a social constructivist perspective, the very idea of global policy making comes about through gradual processes of interpretation and inter-subjective understandings that develop in relation to labelling certain management practices, forms of decision-making, and other public acts as 'global public policy'. The idea of global policy also becomes a tangible reality when it is developed into a focus of research or around university teaching. Ideas, policy experiments and professional experiences become real and meaningful, or a 'fact', as they consolidate or institutionalise in academic thinking, or in 'soft law' and cross-national regulation, or in the understandings developed within transnational policy communities. Labelling phenomena as 'global policy' are 'world-making' (Gergen, 2014) in the sense that a heterogeneous set of words are transformed into a more or less coherent set of concepts that are informed by the lived professional experiences of those using them. But processes of 'world-making' are also permeated with the values and power interests of those policy actors using the terms.

Just as domestic policy making is often an uneven playing field with certain classes or communities gaining privileged access, and others excluded, so too global policy processes reflect global inequalities. One might ask: Is 'global policy' really 'global', or is it 'Western'? The dominance of English as the language of global policy making has already been observed (Moloney and Stone, 2019). The leading international organisations – World Bank, International Monetary Fund (IMF) and OECD amongst others, have long been criticised for being too Western oriented in their policy prescriptions (e.g. see Clifton and Díaz-Fuentes, 2011, depicting the OECD as a 'Club of the Rich'). Those whom international organisations employ, contract or partner with are often Western-educated middle-class professionals, that have been critically tagged in the case of World Bank participatory policies, as a 'comprador class' (Kamruzzaman, 2013) or in the case of the International Standardization Organization (ISO) as 'global rulers' (Büthe and Mattli, 2013). Not unexpectedly, the notion of 'global policy' is often resisted as an elite project.

Not using the term 'global policy' is equally significant. Aversion to such a term at an institutional or group level can signify the presence of institutional interests opposed to the symbolic power that might be accorded to the term 'global policy'. Some political and policy actors might veer away from words like 'global policy' and 'transnational administration' because of the implicit challenge to state sovereignty and other established institutions of public authority or representative government that the words represent. The social order depends on 'sedimented understandings' (Gergen, 2014: 289) – like that of the sovereign state order – which are disrupted by the concepts, practices and instruments of global policy.

The term 'global governance' is the better recognised concept and one that can encompass notions of global, regional or transnational policy. Even so, an artificial divide has persisted in the social sciences between Political Science, Public Administration and Public Policy on one side of conceptual parameters, with the cognate fields of IR, International Political Economy and Security Studies on the other. Disciplinary boundaries have seen the dominance of the concepts of the latter to the detriment of the full development of understanding 'global governance'. The ideas of 'global (public) policy' and 'transnational administration' are ripe for wider inter-disciplinary debate about the contours of global governance. To date, however, many policy scholars have used the term 'global policy' without defining it (inter alia Held and Koenig-Archibugi, 2004; True, 2003).

'Global public policy' has been called 'governing without government' (Reinicke, 1998). Another view considers that 'a policy is "global" to the extent that policy actors operating in a global or transnational space are involved in policy development, transfer, and implementation' (Orenstein, 2005: 180). The phrase 'global policy making' is also used in a limited sense as the international circulation of policy models between countries (Milhorance, 2018). The journal *Global Policy* defines the scholarly field of 'global policy' as one that: 'focuses on the global as a process (or set of processes) that creates transcontinental or interregional flows and networks of activity and interaction, and the new framework of multi-level policy making by public and private actors, which involves and transcends national, international and transnational policy regimes' (Held et al., 2010: 1). Another definition ties 'global policy' to administrative functions:

> *Global (Public) Policy (GPP)* is a set of overlapping but disjointed processes of public-private deliberation and cooperation among both official state based and international organisations with non-state actors around establishing common norms and policy agendas for securing the delivery of global public goods or ameliorating transnational problems.

> *Transnational Administration (TA)* refers to the regulation, management and implementation of global policies of a public nature by both private and public actors operating beyond the boundaries and jurisdictions of the state but often in areas beneath the global level. (Stone and Ladi, 2015)

These few definitions differ considerably in their scope, including whether or not to include the word 'public'. Nevertheless, there are some common themes.

First, decision-making is *polycentric* rather than state-centric (Cerny, 2017). There is no single institutional focus for the formulation and implementation of global public policy. Various actors will be involved. These may include public actors including states and international organisations and private actors of many different kinds. Accordingly, there is more often reference to 'global policy *networks*' as manifestations of global policy (inter alia Orenstein, 2005; Slaughter, 2004).

Second, unlike realms of national policy making where new laws and regulations apply universally, *the implementation of global policies is not necessarily global*. While policy norms and agendas may be designed with global resonance, the pattern of policy implementation, and compliance, varies significantly from one community or country to another. Policy applications can be geographically specific and limited to a few countries. Or made at a regional level or via processes of trans-regionalism (Hoffmann, 2019). This differential pattern often results from policy diffusion processes which can occur between just a few countries (Evans, 2019; Orenstein, 2005: 179).

Third, like nation-state policy making, the boundaries between policy areas are often blurred to the point that it is difficult to determine what agency or organisation, and which private or public actors are responsible for addressing the given problem. Whereas situations like these at the nation-state level might be mitigated by the intervention of executive authorities, no such authorities exist at the global level. In such circumstances, global policy making becomes more protracted as competing sites of authority come into play. Many questions arise about the nature of global policy making and structure the remainder of this section: What does global policy look like? Where is global policy executed? Who is involved? When can it be seen? Why is it important?

What? Global Public Goods?

The concept of GPGs often stands as a proxy for 'global public policy'. For instance, two World Bank authors refer to their Bank as standing 'at the intersection of national and global public policy' but write exclusively of GPGs provision (Evans and Davies, 2014). Economists and other policy researchers at the UN ignited much of the work on GPGs (Kaul and Conceição, 2006; Jenks, 2012). They established a policy agenda subsequently adopted by other international organisations like the European Commission and the World Bank, amongst others (Bodansky, 2012). The patronage of governments and international organisations funding taskforces into the academic analysis, and policy applications, of GPGs theory has, in a recursive process, fuelled practice (Jenks, 2012). 'The growing literature on GPGs has provided new intellectual stimulus to international agencies to implement such global agreements by getting involved in partnerships and financing international public goods' (OED, 2002: 4). The idea of 'global policy' and 'global programmes' became hinged to that of GPGs. In other words, the GPG concept and its policy applications, has been 'world-making'.

Examples of GPGs include a clean environment; a world free from malaria, HIV/AIDS or tuberculosis; and 'knowledge 4 development' such as in the form of readily accessible statistics, research and training. The benefits of such public goods are enjoyed by all; in other words, they are 'non-excludable' on a global scale. By the same stroke, the public is not excluded from 'public bads': these might include the ill effects of a thinning ozone layer and the resulting costs of environmental damage. The world is beset with 'global public bads' that include, amongst many other problems, declining bee populations and fish stocks as well as global and regional financial crises or the mounting problem of 'space junk' orbiting the earth. 'Such goods are, as economists say, public in consumption, meaning they might affect anyone anywhere, for better or worse' (Kaul, 2019: 257). The GPG concept is an ideal-type: In reality most public goods (and bads) are 'impure'. For instance, long thought to be non-rivalrous, public goods such as fresh air, do have a rivalrous quality, as illustrated by pollution concentrated in mega-cities.

The World Bank has long argued that tackling GPGs can only be produced in sufficient supply 'through co-operation and collective action by developed and developing countries' (cited in Agerskov, 2005: 2). However, traditional mechanisms such as treaties and multilateral action are often too slow or beset with political impediments. New institutional tools such as 'informal' international organisations, transnational policy networks or public–private partnerships have emerged mostly in order to counter the effects of public bads but also as mechanisms to facilitate the delivery of public goods. 'TB control is a global "public good"' one World Bank official declares of the Stop TB initiative arguing that, in general, global health is best achieved through strong public–private partnerships (Nishimuzu, 2000).

The justification for these global interventions is that as public goods are non-excludable, they tend to be under-provided, since communities or countries, can free ride on the efforts of others. As GPGs cannot be provided by governments acting unilaterally, international cooperation is needed. But it is often in short supply (Jenks, 2012). Due to the non-rivalrous nature of GPGs, in a world of sovereign nations, no single nation can capture fully the benefit of its own spending on a 'global' good (Birdsall and Diofasi, 2015; Kaul, 2019). In the absence of a 'global sovereign' or a state-like entity capable of enforcing contribution of GPGs by all states, advocates of GPGs frequently call for more international cooperation between states, often through international organisations such as the UN (Boonen et al., 2018: 10).

Whilst a powerful concept in clarifying the cross-border or global character of many contemporary policy problems, the GPG framework does not provide a guide to the allocation of resources; the prioritisation of problems, or the structure and governance of collective action (Kaul, 2019). These policy design issues contain the seeds of political conflict. Many countries, communities and individuals regard climate change as the most pressing global challenge, but for others, disease or illiteracy are paramount policy concerns. Moreover, there is a significant data problem in that governments, international governments and other GPG provides 'have not agreed on any standard definition of GPGs, nor do they report systematically on their own spending' for GPGs through development assistance (Birdsall and Dioffasi, 2015: 5).

Nevertheless, for international organisations that came under considerable criticism at the turn of the millennium, the GPG framework has been a legitimising force for their roles as global policy makers. This is due in some degree to the double entendre of 'global public good':

> In economics, a public good can be normatively good or bad … (but) economists mean only that it is non-rival and non-excludable. In the argument regarding legitimacy, in contrast, the term 'good' is assumed to convey a normative evaluation. 'Global public goods' are contrasted with 'global public bads', rather than seen as encompassing them. That is why global public goods help to provide legitimacy to international institutions: because they are normatively desirable. And that is why the term 'global public goods' has undergone inflation. Recasting an issue in terms of 'global public goods' gives it greater status and thus serves a useful rhetorical function. (Bodansky, 2012: 655)

For example, the SDGs are cast as GPGs, a set of goals lead by the UN and supported by a host of other international organisations and governments (Boonen et al., 2018). But private actors can also finance or deliver public goods.

Global public good delivery by private actors is what some see as a route to private authority in global governance (Eaton and Porter, 2008). Governments may sometimes presume that policy areas are so complex and technically demanding that the private sector – whether it be industry actors or the professions – is best suited for designing appropriate rules and procedures. Or governments might not be willing or able to co-operate to pool sovereignty. In the absence of state collaboration, if economic pressures are intense, private actors may take it upon themselves to set up an international market framework. Such institutions of private authority may not involve governments at all, but still be accepted as legitimate because of the expertise and economic strength of the participants.

These developments are particularly present in the formulation and implementation of regional and global regulatory policies such as in the area of 'transnational merchant law' as well as in the formation of international accounting rules (Eaton and Porter, 2008). Some regard this as the privatisation of regulation in global financial markets, standards setting for financial reporting, global product markets, nanotechnology and other areas seeking standards under the rules of the ISO (Büthe and Mattli, 2013). Although self-regulation and industry 'codes of conduct' can deliver efficiency and effectiveness in many respects, as well some degree of transparency, these developments do raise the question about what is 'public' about global 'public policy'.

Where? The Global Public Sphere

How to characterise the global, regional or transnational spaces in which policy making activities take place entails interrogating the very meaning of terms like 'public' and 'private'. Both of these terms are common distinctions that are made in the study of public policy, and within the legal systems and political economies of nation-states but which are much less amenable to map onto global policy processes.

Numerous ideas have been circulating about the emergence of a global public 'domain' (Drache, 2001; Ruggie, 2015) or global public 'sphere' (Volkmer, 2019) or a global policy 'agora' (Stone, 2013). Some scholars stress the communicative prospects (inter alia Dryzek, 2006). In this regard, global public spheres are 'discursive structures that enable communication beyond state borders' (Mitzen, 2005: 401). Digital networks reach across continents to connect communities in unprecedented ways driving the transformation of public communication in societies worldwide. In this 'deterritorialized public sphere', the traditional dichotomies of 'foreign' and 'domestic' or 'global' and 'national' become far less relevant (Volkmer, 2019: 240). Social and political connections are not restrained by territoriality.

> Not only are communicative spheres increasingly spatially 'disembedded' from national territories but so are – often overlooked – core assets of public civic engagement practices which are now also 'stretched': one can live in Argentina, vote in France, follow the U.S. election campaign 'live' on streaming US or Spanish television websites and engage with climate change issues with activists in Indonesia and direct blog debates with scientists based in Antarctica. (Volkmer, 2019: 242)

In these formulations, the global public sphere is 'characterized by two levels: "transnational" public spheres, constituted by vertical, critical dynamics among non-state actors, and "international" public spheres constituted by horizontal dynamics among states' (Mitzen, 2005: 402).

Sociologist Manuel Castells (2011) gives some institutional flesh to communicative processes in this public sphere with emphasis on networks and civil society. The IR scholar, John Gerard Ruggie (2004: 499) argues that there is an emerging 'global public domain' which provides a 'transnational arena concerned with the production of global public goods'. Other ideas stressing the political and policy dimensions of this domain include the notion of a 'global polity' (Corry, 2010) which is for other observers, specified by three analytical aspects: a set of structured arenas, mechanisms for global policies, and embodiment of relations of power (Ougaard and Higgott, 2002).

Depending on the issue or policy sector vantage point (for instance, migration or corruption issues) and disciplinary orientation, various scholars have stressed specific features of the 'sphere'. These include the deliberative potential of a global public sphere (Dryzek, 2006), its capacity for regulation or rule making (Büthe and Mattli, 2013), its network character (Castells, 2011), and the roles of business (Ronit, 2018) or civil society in global policy delivery. These observations point to a kaleidoscopic set of perspectives where the 'sphere' is conceptually shifting in different reflections on its institutional, legal and policy practice dimensions. Indeed, rather than one sphere, there are multiple public spheres, and subaltern counter-publics who do not fall neatly within the 'Westphalian grammar' of sovereign nation-states (Fraser, 2013).

Regardless of how this sphere might be delineated, it is not a level playing field among states, communities, international organisations, the public, business and civil society – there are significant power disparities and disputes. Real inequalities and ideological differences persist between the advanced market economies and Western(ised) liberal democracies on the one hand, and the disparate, often neo-colonial, experiences of developing countries that are all too frequently lumped together as the 'Global South' (Moloney and Stone, 2019). Moreover, the public–private distinction does not hold in the same manner as it does in context of sovereign nation-state decision-making. Distinctions between public and private are very opaque. Global policy activity is as likely to take place inside private associations among non-state actors as in intergovernmental conferences. There is no single centre of power; rather, there are multiple nodes of policy making. Some nodes, or actors involved in them are more visible or public, whereas other non-state nodes of power and persuasion are more private and exclusive.

The global public sphere is often not a physical space. Rather, it is a space of practices created by the interactions of its actors. Consequently, the shape of the global agora can sometimes be that of a virtual or electronic commons (Volkmer, 2019). With fragmentation of policy responsibilities distributed through networks, the sites of political authority are more devolved. The locations of decision-making are dispersed geographically and often shift between summits and other high-level dialogues in global cities (Sassen, 2016). This situation is in distinction to the clearly demarcated domains of 'public' and 'private' carved out by law and sovereign authority characteristic of most OECD states. Without a global authority structure – the Westphalian dilemma (Kaul, 2019: 267) – public and private becomes entwined.

Traditionally, the rights and responsibilities of 'the public' – as well as the citizen – have been associated with a sovereign order. Yet, the notion of the public is often lost from analytical sight at global, regional and transnational levels. Indeed, the conventional idea of citizenship stops at nation-state borders. The notion of 'global citizenship' is therefore an impractical buzzword which reaches its limits when it comes to operationalisation of the phrase. It is another reason for the greater currency of the term 'global policy' than for 'global *public* policy' given the lack of legal and institutional foundations for global citizenship rights and responsibilities (Moloney and Stone, 2019). Citizens are legally defined as persons with 'the *right* to participate in government and public life' (the legal definition) but also an '*obligation* to participate' (Cooper and Yoder, 1999: 196, original emphasis). There is no neat parallel or inter-operability when applied to the global public sphere (Eriksen and Sending, 2013: 213). Spaces for citizen participation lack the Westphalian-inspired boundaries present within and between sovereign states. While 'the nation-state is not necessarily the most suitable political framework for housing citizenship rights' (Turner, 1993: 178), nevertheless, the public servant, and the notion of civil service, is also tied to the nation-state and its citizens. The insufficient global parallel poses a problem if it is the 'ethical dimension of citizenship that provides the normative foundations for the role of the public administrator' (Cooper and Yoder, 1999: 196). If not citizens, then who is prominent in the making of global public policy?

Who? Transnational Policy Communities

There is a surfeit of labels to describe transnational policy actors and decision-makers: 'international civil servants' or 'supranational bureaucrats' or 'global managers' (Patriota et al., 2013) or 'policy flexians' (Stubbs, 2013) or 'global rulers' (Büthe and Mattli, 2013). Whatever the nomenclature, the key characteristic of 'transnational policy communities' is a mix of public and private actors with differing bases of authority from legal, epistemic, financial, political and bureaucratic sources or experience. When thinking about 'who' is central in global policy processes, there are three main categories of global policy actors, all of who can be regarded as elites in some way:

1. International civil servants. These people are usually employed by an inter-governmental organisation – like UN agencies, the World Bank or the European Commission – to staff its secretariat and institute operations (Newman and Ravndal, 2019; Biermann and Siebenhüner, 2013). These individuals are not state delegates. The conventional paradigm of international civil service includes impartiality, objectivity and international loyalty rather than national particularism. The reality is more complex, where national interests continue to be pursued. Even so, international civil servants have considerable capacity to shape (or delay) policies because of their expertise, routines, and positions of power (Weller and Xu, 2019). However, these individuals and secretariats are relatively 'invisible' to everyday publics. Nevertheless, scholars are fast developing concepts of 'international public administration' (Knill and Bauer, 2018) to account for the bureaucratic autonomy of inter-governmental organisations.

As international civil servants often hold diplomatic status (but not usually locally engaged staff) they are often not studied by policy scholars as bureaucrats and managers within an international public administration (IPA, Trondal, 2016). Yet, as the 'bureaucratic arm' of intergovernmental organisation, the extent to which these bureaucrats design policies of their own and, to some degree, become independent of their member state governments has become increasingly tangible (Bauer et al., 2018). The personal leadership styles of secretary-generals or presidents as well as the recruitment of IPA staff within certain disciplines or professions can create coherence among a bureaucratic cadre of an inter-governmental organisation that generates not only quite different administrative styles among them, and across organisations, but which member states can also find difficult to check. For example, the IMF teaches norms to national officials via transnational policy training to increase the number of domestic reformers who are sympathetic to IMF policy prescriptions (Broome and Seabrooke, 2015). Other organisational factors – source of funding, budgeting processes, mandate, governance structure, human resource policies – are also determining factors of IPA autonomy and hence capacity in creating or influencing global policies (Knill and Bauer, 2018).

2. Internationalised public-sector officials. These are bureaucrats employed by states who regularly interact with other national counterparts on cross-border policy problems through 'global government networks' (Slaughter, 2017). These are sovereignty enhancing arrangements where state policy powers are not diluted but are enhanced through cross-national collaboration among both high-level officials as well as between lower-level national regulators, who act as delegates of national political processes. These networks of judges, legislators or regulators are trans-governmental because state appointed public officials remain the core actor. They are formally designated power holders and rule makers who derive their authority from their official positions within their nation-state.

The changing roles for these state-based public sector officials arises from the 'denationalization of the state'. Saskia Sassen (2016) coins this term to deal with the growing number of national public officials whose work is directed at the ongoing functioning of the global economy. For example, central bank governors, while paid by their respective states, spend significant amounts of time working together both through monthly meetings at Basel, Switzerland and almost daily electronic contacts to address ongoing crises and problems in the global financial system. Public servants focused on the trade regime spend increasingly larger amounts of time meeting on many of the committees of the World Trade Organization (WTO) in Geneva. The roles being played by national public servants in supporting the ongoing functioning of the Group of 20 (G20) or the BRICs are illustrative of how the responsibilities of these officials become increasingly global as opposed to being simply national.

3. Transnational policy professionals. This diverse community includes an array of business leaders and consultants, international philanthropists and foundation officers, scientific experts, think tank pundits and NGO executives who connect transnationally to inform, implement or coordinate policy. Their status as either public or private agents is not always evident. Private consultants are contracted by public bodies, and private experts are co-opted into official advisory bodies. Rather than acting individually, they are usually found in a network or association that is in receipt of public support or patronage.

With regards to high-level elite interaction in policy development, the term 'policy flexian' (Stubbs, 2013) has been deployed to describe the powers of global 'movers-and-shakers' like the billionaire hedge fund philanthropist George Soros or the economist and special UN advisor Jeffrey Sachs. They are represented as global-spanning policy entrepreneurs and power brokers. In general, 'policy flexians' juggle positions and representations that they acquire through their wealth, prestige or high-level networks generating overlapping roles that personalise bureaucracy and privatise information. They 'operate at the nexus of official and private power, crafting and co-opting global policy agendas which they are, then, often asked to implement and/or evaluate' (Stubbs, 2013). Similarly, but at a lower level of day-to-day operations of global policy, are the professionally diverse cadres of technicians, NGO educators, experts and officials who do not attract the same degree of media attention but who are essential to everyday delivery of policy and executing 'transnational administration'.

Although sometimes overlapping with IPA, 'transnational administration' is a broader domain of public action. IPA is restricted to intergovernmental organisation and interactions with states. Transnationally administered arenas are more likely to be de-concentrated rather than 'concentrated' under a hierarchically organised authority structure. Nor does transnational administration need to be anchored in either the administrative state or international organisations. Instead, transnational administration is a decentralised, devolved or delegated interaction via transnational policy communities where network management becomes administrative action.

All three categories of actors interact in varying degree with each other to facilitate policy transfer, transnational regulation and the delivery of GPGs. Their roles as agenda setters, policy entrepreneurs or global policy implementers and their contributions to policy innovation are either distant or rarely open to public scrutiny. Nation-state bureaucracies can usually be controlled by legislatures and political parties or monitored from the bottom up by watchdog groups, interest associations and citizen's movements. In contrast, transnational bureaucracies are not as proximate to societal forces. The political control of bureaucracies is an enduring concern but when it comes to global policy development, there is a hiatus of such control. Looking into the 'black box' of transnational policy communities, it is necessary to consider whether these actors behave substantially differently from their traditional bureaucratic counterparts as a consequence of this slippage of oversight. To date, whether their powers are exercised with similar constraints and accountability has received scant academic attention.

How? Policy Transfer and Trans-governmentalism

Policy moves. The processes by which policy has moved across nations or organisations have gone by different social science labels. This includes the overlapping notions of policy ambassadors (De Oliveira, 2017), policy circulation (Vogelpohl, 2019), policy diffusion (Orenstein, 2005; Milhorance, 2018), policy learning (Meseguer, 2005), policy mobilities (Prince, 2010; Peck and Theodore, 2015), policy transfer (Evans, 2019; Hadjiisky et al., 2017) and policy translation (Stone, 2013). They share the common concern to identify the forces precipitating the movement of policy ideas and instruments across national borders. There are important differences between these concepts but for the sake of simplicity, the discussion below focuses on the policy transfer framework.

Policy transfer is the deliberate international spread of various types of governance knowledge, rules and standards, sometimes called 'soft law' as well as (hard) policy tools, conditional funds, laws and institutional practices. These are actively diffused by private and public individuals, (international) organisations, states and networks (Evans, 2019; Peck and Theodore, 2015). Development of international norms regarding 'best practice' or regulatory standards is now undertaken in the professional deliberations of various sector- or issue-specific transnational policy communities in matters as varied as pension reform (Orenstein, 2005) or tobacco control (Mamudu et al., 2015) or urban policy (Vogelpohl, 2019).

Advocacy of standard setting and harmonisation of practice are also seen in many global programmes of international organisations like the World Bank. Likewise, the OECD has pioneered peer-to-peer review: that is, diffusing policy tools through international teams of experts and experienced bureaucrats who examine and assess the public performance of another state with the ultimate goal of helping the reviewed state improve its policy making, adopt best practices, and comply with established standards and principles (Pal, 2019). These reviews involve the transmission of knowledge and experience as well as various strategies and instruments for cross-national and trans-national learning, such as benchmarking, peer review, twinning programmes, checklists and 'facilitated coordination'.

Clearly, important forces behind policy innovation and reform originate from outside the state. A *transnational* policy transfer perspective not only undermines the temptation to view the forces behind policy change arising from domestic forces but points to aspects of policy design occurring outside state structures and created by private actors. This development is a significant challenge to traditional understanding of sovereignty whereby policy transfer and the transnational circulation of policy models propelled by non-state policy elites – like management consultancy firms (Vogelpohl, 2019) or think tanks (Stone, 2013) – become players in global steering processes (Milhorance, 2018; De Oliveira, 2017).

Trans-governmentalism is one of the main transmission routes for policy transfer. First identified in the 1970s, trans-governmental cooperation is defined as 'direct interactions among governmental subunits not directly controlled or closely guided by policies of the cabinet or chief executive'. That is, domestic officials were increasingly induced to reach out directly to their foreign counterparts in order to deal with policy problems that spilled over national borders. In other words, the phrase '"trans-governmental" applies when we relax the assumption that states act as units' (Keohane and Nye, 1974: 42). Rather than inter-state diplomacy and treaty negotiations – which can be rather time-consuming and often inconclusive – much international policy coordination is undertaken through informal networks. These iterative processes of lower-level 'regularised interaction' among government officials and regulators can produce change in attitudes, reinforced by common professional memberships, leading to further policy coordination (Dawes et al., 2012). In other words, policy learning can take place in trans-governmental networks (Legrand, 2019).

Three decades later in her book *A New World Order*, Anne-Marie Slaughter (2004) identified a growing global matrix of government networks galvanised to confront common transnational policy challenges. Although they bring together officials with significant formal regulatory and legal responsibilities, these networks are 'necessarily informal' arrangements and do not have a legal or treaty-based existence. Well-known examples include the global regulatory role of the Basel Committee on Banking Supervision (Jordana, 2017) or the joint UNDP and OECD initiated Tax Inspectors without Borders to support countries in building tax audit capacity and strengthen international cooperation on tax matters. There are also a range of environmental enforcement networks such as the International Network for Environmental Compliance and Enforcement (Dawes et al., 2012).

Contemporary understandings of policy transfer and especially trans-governmental policy coordination preserve a significant role for state actors. The next section discusses other network types that bring non-state actors directly into global policy making. Nevertheless, the surge this century of policy transfer and trans-governmental dynamics highlight the limitations of 'methodological nationalism' in Policy Studies when it comes to grappling with global dilemmas.

When? Moving to Methodological Transnationalism

'Methodological nationalism' emphasises domestic politics and policy processes *within countries*. The approach is often linked to social research which takes the nation-state to be the most basic (and even natural) organising principle of social and political relations. In both Policy Studies and IR methodological nationalism becomes manifest in the manner in which basic conceptual distinctions are drawn; for example, between the domestic, national or internal on the one hand and then on the other, between foreign, international or external. Methodological nationalism also becomes apparent in how theories are built about and around the state, and in how cases and data are constructed mostly for purposes of comparison among states or for one and the same state over time. Spatial scales are not pre-given or natural arenas of social interaction but are historical products whereby: 'National scale is the historical product of certain social forces, just as transnational scale is a socially and technologically produced achievement that has been partly made possible by, for instance, information technology and the development of transportation' (Kauppinen, 2015: 12).

By contrast, 'methodological transnationalism' not only highlights global problems, international politics and policy processes *cutting across countries* (Yeates, 2014: 2–3) but also how problems are woven between levels of governance. Policy domains become de-territorialised, and in some degree de-linked from states, to function in an autonomous manner that deviates from conventional Westphalian understandings of boundaries. These transnational policy spaces refer to 'sustained concatenation of cross-border ties and (governance) practices' (Faist, 2012: 53), as exemplified, for example, in the inter-connected relationships of international philanthropy, business and international organisation in the global public–private partnerships discussed in the next section.

When the state is treated as the analytical unit and locus of power and authority, or as cartographic territorial units where legalist notions of sovereignty prevail (Strandsbjerg, 2010), understanding of what can constitute the public domain and the remit of public policy is limited. What is missed are the new public spaces that are being carved out by the international activities of governments, business and non-state actors when they are dealing with the proliferation of cross-border policy problems that come with the movement of goods, organisms and information.

Working analytically within a frame of 'methodological transnationalism', neither policy making nor public administration is viewed simply as being the repository of states, or of state actors co-operating internationally. Instead, methodological transnationalism identifies the nation-state as just one of several possible governance frameworks in which to situate policy processes and the public sector. This methodological stance allows us to recognise the interconnectedness of different hierarchical and network structures of both a public and private nature at the transnational, international and/or global level (Stone and Ladi, 2015). Without prejudging the primacy of one of them, this allows analysis of multiple and simultaneous fora of policy making and administrative practice operating across various socio-spatial jurisdictions. This vantage point means that policy scholars can reflect upon spatial concepts which are often implicitly applied in empirical analyses and how the social sciences tend 'to treat the container of the national state as a quasi-natural social and political configuration' (Faist, 2012: 52). Armed with a transnational perspective, it becomes erroneous to assume the congruence of either policy making or the public sector with the territorial boundaries of the nation-state.

> There is no privileged unit or site of analysis from a transnational optic. A transnational methodology has to consider both deterritorialized elements in the form of intense flows across the borders of states and territorial elements in the efforts of states and organizations to control such flows and establish criteria of membership for persons. An appropriate starting point is therefore the concept of transnational social space which includes both a 'space of flows' and a 'space of places'; the former referring to the deterritorialized and the latter to the territorial elements. (Faist, 2012: 54)

Disconcerting as it may be to those of us who have grown up to equate public policy as an artefact of the nation-state and socialised to vest our identity as citizens of local and national governments, the policy making environment has changed. This situation 'implies the need to study the local, national, regional, international and/or transnational administrative bodies, policy groups, (inter) governmental agencies, and/or transnational epistemic communities' which are not neatly nested but articulated in complex patterns and linkages (Kauppinen 2015: 13).

Why? A Global Public Sector

Earlier it was asked: What does global policy look like? The response started with the idea of GPGs and the difficulties in their provision. But global policy making is much more than the financing and provision of GPGs. Over the past three decades, there has been considerable amount new activity and experimental governance with the evolution of international standard setting and 'soft law', the emergence of global taskforces, global public–private partnerships, global policy networks and an enhanced velocity of international summitry. These are public-sector entities that are, in varying degree, publicly steered or publicly funded agencies, enterprises and networks delivering public programmes, goods or services. The very diverse range of policy activity on this front, sponsored not only by international organisations and states as formal authorities, but also by business and other non-state actors like philanthropic foundations and NGOs help to constitute what might be called an emergent 'global public sector'. The network features of this public sector are the subject of the next section.

The usual understanding of the public sector is that the term refers to that sector of the economy providing governmental services, the exercise of public authority or the implementation of public policies as well as businesses and industries that are owned, regulated or otherwise controlled by government. Yet, with the worldwide policy penchant for privatisation and deregulation since the 1990s, the boundaries of the public sector have become more difficult to discern. Conceptually stretching the idea of public sector to 'global sector' is also not straightforward. A global public sector is not simply the consequence of national public-sector agencies internationalising their activities. Rather, a multi-nucleated global public sector is generated by transnational actors. That is, private organisations and civil society actors also create and constitute the global public sector and do so in partnership and collaboration with governments and international organisations. In other words, in the global public sector there is no sovereign or central executive power and authority to issue regulations, finance programmes or enforce implementation. Instead, the origins of global public sectors are more plural – or tri-partite in corporations, government and civil society – as well as dependent on consensus and joint authority.

Although it may be uneven, ill formed and highly differentiated, the public sector takes shape just as much from the 'state-like' *functions*, *powers* and *apparatuses of* transnational networks. These networks – discussed in greater detail in the next section – represent a delegation of public power. Likewise, the joint public–private provision of services, usually regarded as 'public', as well as various other institutional rearrangements witnessed with the growth of '*informal* international organisation', have not only made the identification of the public sector more difficult, but have also generated partially private global components of the public sector.

Conclusion

Traditionally, the field of Policy Studies has been the obverse of IR. Both scholarly domains respect the nation-state as an established conceptual construct of sovereign authority. Where IR addresses relations between states, public policy assesses policy processes inside specific states often by comparing policies in several states (comparative public policy). Traditional IR still struggles to move out of the conceptual shadow of classical geopolitics (Kleinschmidt and Strandsbjerg, 2010), while Policy Studies finds it difficult to leave the shadow of domestic politics. Both fields of inquiry tend to portray the state as constituting socially exclusive 'containers' and they base analysis on a sharp segmentation of territorial units in a cartographic understanding of global politics (Kleinschmidt and Strandsbjerg, 2010). This produces 'methodological nationalism' whereby the state is treated as the locus of power and authority and thus the analytical unit for academic analysis.

If we are to move further in defining and understanding the characteristics of global public policy, we are faced with another question: *Is Policy Studies itself globalising?* Certainly, the scholarly field of Policy Studies has evolved over the past three decades. But it is yet to contribute fully to understanding global governance. The theories and concepts of Public Administration, Public Management and the so-called Policy Sciences have much to offer in analysing governance innovations. The next section turns to some of these instruments, tools and mechanisms of global policy.

There are also significant questions of a normative nature. Is global public policy making a closed and elite endeavour? If so, to what extent, can and should, global public policy be made more democratic, open and accountable? These are perennial questions against which this Elements can do little justice suffice to point out that the phrase 'global policy' is more commonly used than that of 'global *public* policy'. This is because the 'public' is often lost from sight, and the 'citizen' is often displaced by the more limited notion of 'stakeholder'. Moreover, global public policy is not necessarily the consequence of 'public' action. The shorter phrase also recognises that authority becomes more informal and privatised. Settling upon the term 'global policy' embraces the range of possibilities that blend together public and private authority. The increasingly widespread adoption of the phrase 'global policy', by NGOs but also by international organisations like the World Bank and WHO, is not mere rhetoric but transformative and world-making in helping make global policy become a social 'fact'.

3 Transnational Networks: Policy in Partnership

Governments and international organisations are an obvious set of policy players in the global public sector. However, the implementation of global policy making has brought into existence new transnational policy networks and 'global and regional policy partnerships' (GRPPs) to deliver or finance GPGs. There is also the new breed of 'informal' international organisation – like the G20 and BRICs – operating without permanent secretariats (Vabulas, 2019: 401). Since the turn of millennium, there has also been a devolution of authority and governance to a wider range of stake holders and non-state actors. But there is no central authority that the ordinary person can point to as the hub of the global public sector. Instead, there is a bewildering array of 'issue-specific' mini policy making bodies. This is reflected in the long list of acronyms that this monograph needs to use. These acronyms are symptomatic of 'differentiation' developing in the global public sector (Sending, 2019) – a segmentation of public action around fields like global migration policy' or global food policy' or 'global energy policy'. Rather than being able to provide an organisational chart – such as that sometimes provided to visually depict the structure of a national government with hierarchical chains of authority – the global public sector is better depicted as 'multi-nucleated' and scattered through networks. Often this is called 'polycentricity' (Cerny, 2017).

This section distinguishes between the different types of transnational policy networks. At the 'private' end of the network spectrum, Transnational Advocacy Networks (TANs) have firm footing in civil society and social movements. By contrast, Transnational Private Regulation (TPRs) connect more strongly to business actors and specific industries developing regulatory standards. At the 'public' end of the spectrum are trans-governmental networks (TGNs). In between are transnational public–private partnerships (TPPPs) incorporating a limited selection of private actors forming alliances with counterpart public actors in government and international organisation. And cross-cutting all of them are knowledge networks (KNETs). These KNETs can occasionally become network manifestations of epistocracy.

The World Bank has sponsored many 'global and regional partnership programs'. The UN has patronised the development of 'multi-stakeholder partnerships'. These alliances or partnerships go by different names: For instance, the World Bank has been deeply involved with the 'Consultative Group on International Agricultural Research', the Global Gas Flaring Reduction Initiative as well as the 'Affiliated Network on Social Accountability and Governance in South Asia' (on anti-corruption measures) and dozens of others. UN bodies are connected with initiatives like the Global Handwashing Partnership and the Global Mercury Partnership. More generally, the 2030 Agenda for Sustainable Development call to revitalise the global partnership for sustainable development, tasks the UN Office for Partnerships with responsibility to serve as a 'gateway' for multi-stakeholder partnerships that mobilise and share knowledge, expertise, technology and financial resources towards achievement of the Goals.

There is considerable overlap between the concept of TPPP and that of GRPP. The acronym TPPP is commonly used in the academic literature whereby transnational public–private partnerships are understood as 'a hybrid type of governance, in which nonstate actors co-govern along with state actors for the provision of collective goods, and thereby adopt governance functions that have formerly been the sole authority of sovereign states' (Schäferhoff et al., 2009). The World Bank has a preference for the acronym GRPP regarding the partnership practices they engage in while the UN system tends towards using the phrase 'multi-stakeholder partnership' (Hoxtell, 2017; Martens, 2007). TPPPs will be used in the discussion here as a specific, highly institutionalised sub-category of 'transnational policy network'. But just as international organisations vary in size, structure, policy remit and stature, so too networks are quite different.

The Network Maze of Global Policy Making

As authority over political, social and economic activity is diffused globally among a variety of public and private actors, different varieties of transnational policy networks have become contributors to, and coordinators in, global policy making (Kingah et al., 2015; Slaughter, 2015). Transnational policy networks have been defined as: 'multilateral policy deliberative and policy generating fora composed of government officials (including officials of IOs), NGOs and even corporate partners that engage in initiatives marked by a consensus based decision-making process that is not clad in binding legal treaty-based provisions' (Kingah et al., 2015: 234). This is a broad definition designed, like many other definitions (inter alia Andonova, 2017; Reinicke and Deng, 2000), to encapsulate the great diversity of network participants. However, this definition excludes two varieties of network – those of a purely trans-governmental character, and those transnational networks that are exclusively private and do not include (officially at least) actors from government or international organisation.

It is important to distinguish between the different varieties of policy networks as their power and authority differ, and hence the capacity to shape policy varies considerably. Their composition and structure can also vary significantly depending on the public or private character. The main types of transnational policy networks are summarised in Table 1. Knowledge networks are discussed later in Section 4 suffice to say here that they can become locations for episto-cratic development. These networks incorporate professional bodies, research groups and scientific communities that organise around a scientific interest to provide expertise and evidence for governments and international organisations and are sometimes drawn into diplomacy.

TANS are recognised by their normative ambitions and advocacy orientation. TANs accommodate a range of NGOs and activists and while they can have significant impact on agenda setting (such as the effect of the Nobel Prize–winning International Campaign to Ban Landmines), they are located in global civil society. TANs are bound together by shared values or 'principled beliefs' and a shared discourse. Their 'advocates plead the causes of others or defend a cause or proposition' (Keck and Sikkink, 1998: 8). These networks are norm based. Examples include the transnational campaigns surrounding issues like gender-mainstreaming (True, 2003) as well as policies concerning tobacco, infant formula and pharmaceuticals (Andia and Chorev, 2017; Mamudu et al., 2015). Compared to other network varieties, TANs are like 'outsider groups', as they exercise 'voice' and seek to raise public consciousness on issues to effect policy change, taking full advantage of technological advances in communications that allows the rapid sharing of information and global calls to civic action. Their power arises from moral and ethical persuasion, and their capacity to mobilise public opinion or civic action.

TPRs are also private and composed of non-state actors willing to commit to self-regulatory norms and rules in a given issue area. Rather than forming

Table 1 Transnational Network Types

Network Type	Acronym	Source of Authority	Example	Public–Private Spectrum
Transnational advocacy networks	TANs	Normative authority and the power of moral and ethical persuasion	International Campaign to Ban Landmines; Human rights advocacy networks; Environmental advocacy networks	Private; loosely structured associations with a civil society or social movement location and character
Transgovernmental networks	TGNs	Political authority; government appointees, international civil servants or other officially appointed government representatives	Tax Inspectors without Borders; Basel Committee on Banking Supervision; Pharmaceutical Inspection Cooperation Scheme	Public; loosely structured, peer-to-peer ties developed through frequent communication among specialised domestic officials and regulators
Knowledge networks	KNETs	Epistemic authority from (social) scientific knowledge or training to provide evidence and expertise	Global Development Network (GDN) of think tanks; Consultative Group on International Agricultural Research	Mix of public- and private-sector experts and scientists based in academies, laboratories, think tanks, universities and other knowledge organisations

Transnational private regulation	TPRs	Authority from multi-stakeholder market-based regulatory coordination or standard setting	Forest Stewardship Council International Social and Environmental Accreditation and Labelling Alliance	Private; often operating with governmental recognition of regulatory function
Transnational public–private partnerships	TPPPs	Collective authority derived from resource inter-dependencies and bargaining in a formal partnership of state, market and societal stakeholders to a global problem	UNEP Global Mercury Partnership Stop TB Global Alliance for Improved Nutrition (GAIN)	Voluntary associations of members that is non-binding under international law

around shared values, TPRs emerge from common interests and the shared quandary of market-based problems. Transnational private regulators issue standards in areas as diverse as the environment, sustainability, anti-corruption and legality, human rights, data protection, product safety, and financial instruments and are often complemented by the hard or soft law produced by international organisations and by nation-states (Cafaggi, 2019: 600). Examples are environmental management systems or certification of sustainable fisheries that seek to bind multi-national companies (MNCs) to specific standards of due diligence or codes of conduct in production processes or management of global supply chains. The Forest Stewardship Council is a prominent example of a multi-stakeholder initiative in global forests governance (EEA, 2011: 10). This Council joined forces with several other standard setting bodies in social accountability or ecosystems management to form in 2002 the International Social and Environmental Accreditation and Labelling Alliance now known as the ISEAL Alliance (Cafaggi, 2019: 601). The authority basis of TPRs among participants rests on the claims to efficiency and effectiveness that arise from cooperation and coordination as well as standard setting. The major challenge they face is ensuring compliance.

These two types of network – TANs and TPRs – are not the primary focus of this monograph. This is not to say these two varieties of network are not important or influential. Quite clearly, agenda setting through global civil society activism has been effective in raising consciousness and making controversial matters like 'child soldiers' and 'blood diamonds'. Likewise, private regimes pay respect and respond to consumer clout and concerns about products harming the environment, contributing to climate change or undermining core labour standards (EEA, 2011). However, the concern in this Elements volume is to mark out some of the agencies of what might come to be at the centre of a 'global public sector'. TANs and TPRs are primarily private in constitution. They do not have direct *formal* funding and *official* participation from government actors that makes tangible the 'public' in global public sector. The focus is on (1) TPPPs/GRPPs as issue or sector-specific institutional arrangements for the financing or implementation of GPGs and (2) the trans-governmental policy coordination practices and regulatory power of TGNs.

Adopting a network approach entails 'a focus on practices' (Pouliot and Thérien, 2018: 163) and is well suited to 'methodological transnationalism'. Such an approach is better able to bring into sight a myriad of informal processes in global policy making which complement 'rule-bound' procedures associated with treaties and international organisation. While harder to track analytically, these informal processes 'constitute a critical component ... for debating, negotiating and deciding upon global policies' (Puliot and Therien,

2017: 164). Another advantage of focusing upon networked global policy making is that it allows a more nuanced appreciation of the multiple routes for the pursuit of policy power, as well as the dynamics of exclusion, in the global order.

It is worthwhile distinguishing 'transnational policy networks' from regional economic integration which has some network characteristics. The EU as the most institutionalised regional project is best seen as an international organisation even though it is permeated by numerous issue-specific networks. China's Belt and Road initiative is also a case where regional integration is ostensibly used as a vehicle for alliance building. However, China's Belt and Road initiative is also a state-led trade and infrastructure mega-project of the Chinese government to which other governments choose to join. That is, it is a major inter-governmental project at the macro-level of governance and economic integration. By contrast, the policy networks discussed in this Elements volume are issue and sector specific at the meso-level of analysis and policy practice. For example, the Regional Knowledge Network on Forest Law Enforcement and Governance in the Association of South East Asian Nations (ASEAN) is focused on forestry and agriculture.

Trans-governmental Action

TGNs are designed as a contemporary reconfiguration of sovereignty and extension of state power. TGNs are not based in civil society, as is the case with the TANs, or overlapping into it as do TPPPs (see below). Instead, they are strategic devices for states to extend their public authority beyond borders. These networks are almost exclusively composed of 'internationalised public-sector officials'. As put by another observer, 'trans-governmental interactions are distinct activities insofar as they operate exclusive of non-policy officials, are separate from foreign/diplomacy institutions, and deploy collectively their separate domestic formal authorities and resources to achieve common outcomes' (Legrand, 2019: 204). Similarly, the OECD describes TGNs as 'cooperation based on loosely-structured, peer-to-peer ties developed through frequent interaction rather than formal negotiation, involving specialized domestic officials (typically regulators) directly interacting with each other' (OECD, 2019).

In these networks, the state is un-furled beyond its borders via cross-national connections among 'high level officials directly responsive to the national political process – the ministerial level – as well as between lower level national regulators' (Slaughter, 2004: 19). These are networks of, for example, judges adjudicating on international tax issues or legislators developing new laws for policy coordination on thorny policy matters like foreigners adopting babies and children from countries other than their own, or wicked problems like cross-border criminal activity. The relationships are inter-governmental. The state remains core as a sovereign actor. Those who participate in TGNs are formally designated power holders and rule makers who derive their authority from their official positions within the public bureaucracies of their nation-state.

An underlying assumption behind some TGNs is that networked threats – such as those that come from arms dealers, drug smugglers, human traffickers, money launderers or terrorists – require networked responses. For example, in the 1990s the Financial Action Task Force (FATF) was created as a response to cross-border money laundering (Slaughter, 2004: 6). Networks become tools for the maintenance of sovereignty where global problems are solved by 'networked government' collaboration. Accordingly, TGNs are the most public type of network discussed in this volume.

TGNs are not necessarily 'global' in reach but can be organised regionally, or around a geographically specific policy problem or yet again, around language and cultural groups such as with Francophone or Nordic networks. Since 2001, an extraordinary Anglosphere TGN architecture has grown 'to cover thirty-six networks and subnetworks (exclusive to Australia, Canada, New Zealand, the UK and the USA), involving ~140 departments, agencies or regulatory authorities and ~1500 Anglosphere policy officials in the policy domains of justice, borders and immigration and in security' (Legrand, 2019: 210). One of these is the self-styled 'Quintet of Attorneys-General', which is linked to subsidiary networks in policing, such as the 'Five Eyes Law Enforcement Group', 'Criminal Intelligence Advisory Group'; 'Money Laundering Group'; and the 'Cyber Crime Working Group'.

The OECD claims that 'trans-governmental networks are multiplying fast. But they vary widely in their constituency, governance structure and operational mode'. Just four examples that the OECD (2019) highlights include:

- the Pharmaceutical Inspection Cooperation Scheme (PIC/S) for the 'maintenance of mutual confidence, the exchange of information and experience in good manufacturing practices and the mutual training of Inspectors';
- the European Public Administration network composed of the Directors General responsible for Public Administration in the Member States of the EU;
- the Basel Committee on Banking Supervision; and

- the International Association of Insurance Supervisors (IAIS), which represents regulators in circa 190 countries and issues global insurance 'principles', 'standards' and 'guidance papers' under its remit.

TGNs are also apparent at regional levels. Some have long claimed that 'transgovernmental relations constitute the most important process of integration' in the EU (Thurner and Binder, 2009). Likewise, ASEAN policy makers have made explicit strategic and political claims for the advantages of transgovernmental network arrangements, particularly in environmental issues (Elliott, 2012).

TPPPs: Programmes for Global and Regional Policy

Policy partnerships are also proliferating. Although they have been prevalent at national levels of governance for much longer (Hodge and Greve, 2018), TPPPs have seen barely three decades of experimentation. They are distinctive for their focus on a specific global policy challenge – a shared policy concern like promoting the hygiene benefits of handwashing or reducing gas flaring noted earlier. In other words, TPPPs are defined by shared material interests and partnership principles in delivering public goods. These networks have trisectoral composition, that is, they are alliances of government agencies and international organisations with MNCs, business associations and elements of civil society. Their interactions are shaped by resource dependencies and bargaining. TPPPs are voluntary associations in that membership is nonbinding under international public law (Andonova, 2017: 9). Even so, the official participation of public actors gives some 'insider' status and public authority to TPPPs. They can be thought of as transnational bureaucracies given that they pursue public objectives and receive governmental and other forms of official funding and support. Generally, they are established as 'a new organization with a governance structure and a management unit to achieve its goals' (DAC Network on Evaluation, 2014: 1).

Most TPPPs are housed inside multilateral organisations, in particular the World Bank and UN agencies. Usually global programmes and partnerships are managed by a secretariat of appointed officials – oftentimes staffed by international civil servants or other seconded government actors – as well as various experts and other professionals. In most cases, a global or regional programme is overseen by a board composed of stakeholders such as the representatives of public and private donors, and international organisation. These programmes have decision-making authority over financial allocations and they administer specialised functions for the cross-national delivery of public goods and services.

There are three main types (Beisheim and Simon, 2018: 3): First, TPPPs that share knowledge. For example, the Global Development Network of think tanks and research institutes which are focused on development issues (Stone, 2013). Second, TPPPs that provide goods and services, like cheaper access to vaccines in the case of GAVI. And third, TPPPs that develop regulation or international standards. For example, the UNEP Global Mercury Partnership concerning the release of mercury and its compounds into the environment (Sun, 2017). In short, TPPPs are transnational administrative agencies and are not unlike government agencies or non-departmental public bodies (better known as *quangos*) that operate at national and sub-national levels of governance, albeit with higher levels of private-sector involvement.

Putting a number on these innovations is a challenging data exercise. One OECD estimate puts the number in the 'several hundreds' (DAC, 2014: 1). A 2007 report for the Friedrich Ebert Stiftung dodged the issue by saying that it 'depends, of course, on the definition of the term one uses in identifying them' (Martens, 2007: 20). Nevertheless, this report noted that in connection to the 2002 Johannesburg Summit on Sustainable Development, 164 global partnerships were created while the 'Global Forum for Health Research database contains 92 international partnerships, just in the health sector' (Martens, 2007: 20).

A 2006 UNDP publication, *Global Public Finance* (Kaul and Conceição, 2006), identified around 400 partnerships. A decade later, sampling just four international organisations – the World Bank, UNEP, UNICEF and the WHO, and working with a tight definition of TPPP – another study records 347 entities (Andonova, 2017). A report by GPPi on Multi-Stakeholder Partnerships (Hoxtell, 2017), evaded quantifying the scale of TPPPs focusing instead, on the pressing issues of management and oversight that their increasing numbers were presenting for donors and governments. While TPPP numbers in the global public sector are quite small compared to the extent of quango proliferation and 'agencification' in the public sectors of many OECD countries, their numbers are clearly on the rise.

Institutional growth and development of TPPPs is quite variegated creating an unbalanced or 'patchy' global public sector. Many are seen to have emerged in the environmental policy sector (Andonova, 2017). In another review, around 100 global health initiatives were catalogued whereas in the field of 'global food security' only seven initiatives were identified (Kaan and Liese, 2011: 386–7). These seven include bodies like the Global Alliance for Improved Nutrition (GAIN), the Iodine Network and the Flour Fortification Initiative, Safe Supply of Affordable Food Everywhere, the Farmers Forum, the Ending Child Hunger and Under-nutrition Initiative (now known as REACH) and the International

Alliance Against Hunger – to give a taste of the extent of differentiation of TPPP global policy responsibilities.

Settling upon an agreed definition has been difficult for scholars and practitioners alike. Harkening to their public goods orientation, TPPPs have been defined very broadly as 'multisectoral networks that bring together governments, business and civil society, that is, as institutionalized transboundary interactions between public and private actors which aim at the provision of collective goods' (Bäckstrand et al., 2012: 126). Other definitions also stress (1) the combination of actors from the state, the business sector and society in non-hierarchical relationships (Kaan and Liese, 2011: 386); (2) a degree of institutionalisation through partners conforming around regular communication and consultation and agreed decision-making processes (Schneiker and Joachim, 2018: 2); and (3) sharing of risks and responsibilities related to a specific problem or policy area. For example, the World Bank (IEG, 2007: xvi) defines its 'global and regional programs' as having the following characteristics:

- The partners contribute and pool resources (financial, technical, staff, and reputational) towards achieving agreed-upon objectives over time.
- The activities of the programme are global, regional, or multi-country (not single-country) in scope.
- The partners establish a new organisation with a governance structure and management unit to deliver these activities.

The establishment of an entirely new organisation and a standing secretariat sets TPPPs apart from the looser government sanctioned network interactions of TGNs.

From the turn of the millennium, the United Nations Foundation supported a considerable amount of analytical work and evaluation of partnership programmes. The Foundation is not only advocating the partnership approach but also pioneering praxis. Early advocacy included path-breaking books on this governance innovation (Reinicke and Deng, 2000) as well as reports and guidelines (UNF, 2002). Policy practice at the UN Foundation has meant launching a number of initiatives, mostly in the context of the SDGs or in tandem with other UN bodies. This includes the Global Partnership for Sustainable Development Data, the seven 'food' initiatives mentioned earlier as well as other specialised partnerships like the handwashing and mercury initiatives.

As a governance innovation, many are still weakly institutionalised. But a few have consolidated as permanent structures of governance. The most notable example to be found in the global health policy field is GAVI. When established in 2000, it was known as the Global Alliance for Vaccines and Immunisation. A sign of its success is that it is today best known by its acronym.

At the time its creation, GAVI was a unique public–private partnership, bringing together key UN agencies, governments, the vaccine industry, private sector and civil society to improve childhood immunisation coverage in poor countries and to accelerate access to new vaccines. This model was designed to leverage not only financial resources but expertise as well. Depicted as 'a 21st century development model for a new millennium and one which works', this TPPP claimed in 2017 that GAVI had reached 'over 690 million children since its creation and preventing more than 10 million future deaths in the process' (GAVI, 2019). A large part of its success has been the long-term support of the Bill and Melinda Gates Foundation (Harrow and Jung, 2019).

Established in 1971 the Consultative Group for International Agricultural Research (CGIAR) is one of the oldest and largest global partnership programmes. CGIAR unites organisations engaged in research for a food-secured future focusing on issues such as rural poverty, human health and nutrition and sustainable management of natural resources. By contrast, at the other end of the spectrum of institutional longevity, the World Commission on Dams existed briefly from 1998 to 2001. A sunset clause was built into its legal constitution, but such a clause is unusual in other TPPPs. Most seek to grow and consolidate their existence. As noted in one EU report, 'Where transnational networks assume a more institutionalised form and begin to set norms and rules for their members or other concerned actors, *they become transnational governance institutions in their own right*' (EEA, 2011: 9, my emphasis). It is not unlike 'agencification' seen in national public sectors.

At the national level of policy making, public–private partnerships have become a well-established instrument of service delivery and policy implementation (Hodge and Greve, 2018). However, there important differences to observe between partnerships operating at domestic and international levels. First, the centralised oversight and accountability mechanisms that a government can impose at the national level is significantly diluted in regional and global contexts. Second, there is a lack of a 'coherent demos' where responsibility questions asked by an electorate or its representatives might be raised such as when TPPPs start to fail or show significant inefficiencies (Hodge and Greve, 2018).

Informal International Organisation, Global Task Forces and Summitry

There are other policy practices which are also points in the multi-nucleated global policy sphere. Global dialogues, eminent persons groups or taskforces are 'short-term gatherings' often of a multi-stakeholder character. International organisations like the UN and the World Bank have taken a lead role in convening global conferences around a global concern. These include the Rio conferences on the environment and the Global Task force on GPGs amongst many others (Bäckstrand and Kylsäter, 2014). But there are also privately constituted fora to which policy flexians flock: The World Economic Forum (WEF) convening many of the world's leading political, business and civil society figures in the luxury ski resort of Davos each year is the most notable (Ronit, 2018: 41). Another is the Doha Forum which has convened 'leading figures in policy' with select media groups, think tanks and universities. Also, the Global Drug Commission mimics the style of UN conferences to give it a patina of authority (Alimi, 2015).

Another important feature of the global policy sphere is the proliferation of informal intergovernmental institutions (IIGOs). These are explicit but non-legal arrangements where states regularly interact but do so outside any permanent organisational structure. They have no independent standing secretariat (Vabulas, 2019). That is, bodies like the G20 notable for its international headline grabbing summits, and which many observers suggest has evolved into a 'global steering committee' (Crump and Downie, 2018). Less well known IIGOS include the Alliance of Small Island States, an association allowing small island states to publicise their plight in the face of rising waters from global warming and climate change. Or the Visegrad Four, a forum created by the Czech Republic, Hungary, Slovakia and Poland when seeking entry into the EU addressing common issues such as agriculture, the environment, and energy (Vabulas, 2019) now meeting irregularly to concoct alternative, arguably 'illiberal', visions of the European project.

Finally, programmatic multi-donor trust funds (MDTFs) often function without formal governing bodies (DAC, 2014). MDTFs are financial instruments to hold donor funds 'in trust' and are designed to 'avoid the risk of dispersion': That is, of spreading valuable resources for the SDGs too thinly across too many issue areas. In other words, trust funds are a financial instrument for policy coordination and are often the route through which funds are dispersed to TPPPs. They represent a 'treasury' apparatus for global policy making.

The preceding discussion has drawn out the maze of global policy making – honing onto TGNs and especially global partnership initiatives – but depicting these network innovations embedded in the wider landscape of global policy. In the real word, there is quite a bit of blurring between network types. For example, the G20 is an informal international organisation but it is also interspersed by an array of networks that the G20 itself has encouraged into existence (Slaughter 2015): for instance, Think20 (of think tanks) and Business20 (of business representatives) are usually classified as civil society.

But the degree of government sponsorship or co-option of T20 or B20 can mean that some participating actors have trans-governmental features. Unsurprisingly, the elite composition of the transnational policy networks orbiting the G20 has generated criticism (Slaughter, 2015). The G20 and the networks surrounding it have been portrayed as components of a 'transnational power bloc'. Historical materialist renderings of global policy dynamics as manifestations of a 'transnational state' 'suggests a hegemonic project … centred on the global expansion of industrial capital and modern agriculture' (Ougaard, 2018: 140). However, networks are not always efficient or effective.

Network Effectiveness

There is no perfection in network innovation. These are messy processes characterised by 'trial and error'. Experimentalist governance is a cognate idea here (De Búrca et al., 2014). Networks are flawed. And partnerships – as one type of policy network – can be poorly managed and many are known to have limited or perverse outcomes (Pattberg and Widerberg, 2016).

Networks acts as a gateway in the sense of being an interlocutor between intellectual and policy interests as well as between government and the public. However, networks also become part of gate-keeping processes. In order to gain entry to a specific transnational policy network, any organisation or individual needs to have either official standing or recognised expertise and professional credentials. In general, the critics point to how networks can be exclusionary and elite (GPF, 2014; Heemskerk et al., 2016; Tsingou, 2015). And inside networks, socialisation forces come into play. Networks cultivate the common understandings about the causes and solutions to their set of policy problems that operate as a 'social glue' internally but which also demarcate the boundaries of the network. As such, not only network practices, but also the network analytical approach is epistocratic in essence in that network analysis is a model of elites, for elites, by elites.

Nevertheless, it is important to keep in sight the benefits of networks. As social technologies, networks are a form of socialisation where learning can take place among participants leading to the formation of new policy consensus around which global policy action can take place. Compared to the bureaucracy of large organisations like government departments or UN agencies and the European Commission, networks are usually not bound by the same degree of bureaucratic inertia. They are flatter, less hierarchical and presumed to be faster moving in their ability to respond to global policy problems. Networks are usually more porous to societal participation even if they are dominated by elite actors. Finally, policy networks are infrastructure to 'bridge the local and the global', the multi-levels of governance, by providing connective infrastructures to facilitate cross-national and regional cooperation and policy coordination.

Partnerships: Praise and Pitfalls

'Partnership pundits' laud the benefits. Such benefits include the democratic enhancement of global policy development with the inclusion of a range of civil society actors (Stibbe et al., 2018). The UN publication *Critical Choices* listed half a dozen advantageous features of TPPPs for managing the challenges of globalisation (Reinicke and Deng, 2000). First, like TANS, they are effective at placing new issues on the global agenda (see also Machachek, 2018). They raise global consciousness of pressing problems such as global gas flaring or the health benefits of campaigns by bodies like GAIN or the Global Handwashing Partnership. Second, TPPPs in common with TGNs, are effective instruments to negotiate and set global standards; they function as fora that convene a range of stakeholders to negotiate cooperation in fields as diverse as environmental management or money laundering. Third, as the next section outlines, TPPPs often gather and disseminate evidence and scientific expertise. Fourth, the UN authors argue that private-sector participation helps make TPPPs tools for creating and deepening markets; that is, a mechanism to manage the gap between demand and supply in provision of GPGs. For example, GAVI or the Medicines for Malaria venture encourage pharmaceutical companies to provide anti-malarial and other vaccines at lower cost. Fifth, with public-sector sponsorship, TPPPs are mechanism for policy implementation of inter-governmental treaties as well as providing monitoring and evaluation. Finally, a number of proponents (Kaul and Conceição, 2006) consider that TPPPs help close participatory gaps in the global public sphere by providing additional vehicles for public participation and policy spaces for building not only communication channels but also social capital and trust, and through their public–private nature, a more inclusive process.

'Partnership pessimists' draw attention to the some of the failings: limited accountability; hollowing out of state capacity; and the exclusivity of TPPPs (inter alia Machacek, 2018). Where the pundits identify the potential of TPPPs to increase participation, the pessimists point to the social practices of these transnational bodies to limit the range of participants and exclude certain issues and agendas. That is, entrenched 'ideational pre-alignments' among core participants function 'to decide who is allowed in . . . and who is out' (Schneiker and Joachim, 2018: 3). Accordingly, the pessimists tend to favour the term 'club governance'; such analyses dispute the pluralist argument that TPPPs represent venues for the exchange of ideas and forum for negotiation among participants with different interests and norms in a policy field (Schneiker and Joachim, 2018; regarding KNETs, see Tsingou, 2015). Instead, TPPPs are said to be characterised by 'normative homogeneity' attracting those who already share a common world view to the exclusion of dissident voices (Pouliot and Thérien, 2018: 171).

Relatedly, the advent of these smaller and sector-specific venues of policy can allow greater scope for powerful states to exert unilateral power (Murphy-Gregory and Kellow, 2016: 47–8). Power asymmetries emerge alongside concerns for transparency and accountability. The 'increasing fragmentation of global governance; the weakening of representative democracy and institutions' is a negative outcome warns the Global Policy Forum, a NGO that fears 'the role of the state as primary duty-bearer for guaranteeing the human rights of its citizens . . . is lost through the multi-stakeholder approach' (cited in Besheim and Simon, 2018: 5). Applying the 'bureau-shaping' model of bureaucracy (Dunleavy, 2014) to TPPPs is yet to be done, but this approach is suggestive that network managers will not necessarily want to maximise their budgets, but instead to seek to shape their agency so as to maximise their personal utilities from their work. Such transnational 'empire-building' traits further distance TPPPs, and other network administrations, from locally rooted communities.

In many of the reports produced by or commissioned for UN agencies there is dissatisfaction with the unfulfilled promise of partnership programmes, particularly in developing countries (GPF, 2014; Martens, 2007; Hoxtell, 2017). While partnerships can successfully provide services even in fragile states and conflict-prone areas, relatively few do so. Most partnerships are financed from OECD countries and implemented in middle income countries. Moreover, TPPPs have been criticised as having limited capacity to promote systemic change because 'they tend to focus on specific short-term quantifiable results and thereby detract funding from long-term investment, their ad hoc nature and focus on specific issues may make it difficult to link them to the priority needs of developing countries' (Besheim and Simon, 2016: 5). This is compounded by inadequate provision for 'proper and consistent evaluation of these programs' (UNF, 2002). Moreover, it is often unclear what body has responsibility for managing oversight and accountability of TPPPs (Hoxtell, 2017).

As the UN Foundation notes: 'Partnerships are not painless. They often involve melding different cultures and always imply significant investments of time, and compromises' (UNF, 2002: 4). Unsurprisingly, experimentation with TPPPs can entail mistakes, waste and misalignment of resources. More to the point, however, is the question whether the flourishing of these new governance arrangements makes it either easier or more difficult to manage global policy problems.

The mixed results and effectiveness of TPPPs is backed up in academic studies (Andonova, 2017; Kaan and Liese, 2014; Machacek, 2018). Academic studies tend to bring a further set of systemic concerns that come with the increasing complexity of global and regional governance issues and policy spaces. This includes opportunities for 'forum-shopping'. 'By offering a selection of possible governing sites' – with the flowering of transnational policy networks and IIGOs – there are more venues for 'state and non-state actors to advance their policy goals' (Murphy-Gregory and Kellow, 2016: 41), hence the 'shopping' metaphor. Debate still rages as to whether this allows for healthy competition of ideas that fuels policy development and regulatory experimentation, or whether fragmentation and in-coherence results (Pattberg and Widerberg, 2016). Some point out the negative side effects of private-sector involvement: Rather than plurality, they see fragmentation of global governance and the redesigning of public policies according to private interests rather than public needs (Besheim and Simon, 2016: 5; also Martens, 2007; Yu et al., 2017). A logic is introduced that favours market forms of organisation over and above the public interest. Others have claimed that the privatisation of global governance is overstated (Andonova, 2017). Governments retain significant advantages and controls over policy. Moreover, trans-governmental arrangements which are arguably a more extensive phenomena can be seen as an anti-dote to the 'privatising ethos' of TPPPs or TPRs.

It remains an open question whether public actors drive the policy design of TPPPs or whether there is a dominance of 'PPP solutions promoted by private sector corporations' (Hodge and Greve, 2018: 9). Whatever the case, the long-term contracting, financial flows and secretariat formation mean that TPPPs do become governing regimes. Alongside TGNs, 'they function at the level of both states and global institutions to politically, juridically and ideologically restructure governance forms' (Machacek, 2018: 210). But a critical difference is the character of the public sphere in which transnational PPPs operate compared to PPPs at national and sub-national levels.

The growth of formal partnerships and networks are transforming the multi-lateral institutions with whom they partner and network. This kind of change is endogenous to broader processes of global policy. Or in other words, the networks and partnerships, alongside summits and other transnational dialogues have a generative effect of gestating the global public sector. These processes are not just social technologies to be explained merely as outcomes of collective action around global and regional problems. Instead, these processes have structuring effects of their own; that is, they are 'world-making'. When these processes become normalised – as a recognised tool of governance or an established way of doing things – they become 'socially productive' (Gergen, 2014) fuelling new possibilities for the global public sector and experimentalist governance. Focusing on the financing of GPGs and mechanisms like TPPPs, or the body of practitioner guidelines and consultancy services now evolving around them (Besheim and Ellersiek, 2017: 22–4), 'the often unwritten yet patterned ways of doings things that form the backbone of everyday global public policy making' come into high relief (Pouliot and Thérien, 2018: 164). While, 'the logic behind transnational multistakeholder partnership is attractive for addressing' many of the world's 'wicked problems', the utilisation of this tool is yet to reach its full potential in global public-sector management (Pattberg and Widerberg, 2016: 48).

Diplomacy as Global Policy

With governments and international organisations as partners in TPPPs, or international civil servants as official actors in other transnational policy networks, there are significant implications for the practice of diplomacy. One likelihood is that 'the boom in multi-stakeholder partnerships is a sign of a crisis of purely intergovernmental diplomacy' (Martens, 2007: 6). A seismic shift has already taken place in the move from Westphalian-inspired assumptions of diplomacy being undertaken by political leaders, their staff and diplomats housed in Ministries of Foreign Affairs (MFAs) to contemporary notions of cultural diplomacy, economic diplomacy, science diplomacy and even vaccine or water diplomacy (Cull, 2008; Pamment, 2013). In these specialised contexts, a range of other state and non-state actors take a place, usually a subsidiary one, alongside traditional diplomatic actors. Digital technology also changes diplomatic practice.

Through their cross-border policy work, networks are propelled into the diplomatic landscape where the network organisation not only becomes a potential venue for diplomacy but the network itself can become a diplomatic agent. For example, a report of the European Environment Agency (EEA) considers that the multi-stakeholder model is an ideal tool for allowing consultation and information flows between EU representatives, the Commission and non-state actors. It allows the Commission and the European External Action Service (EEAS) 'to move foreign policy making from its traditional hierarchical model to a network model of international and transgovernmental policymaking' (EEA, 2011: 18).

Three possible future trajectories have been identified for diplomacy due to the growing presence of 'new diplomats' in TPPPs specifically, and transnational policy communities in general:

- Traditional modalities of diplomacy become enmeshed within broader processes of global governance, and diplomacy 'withers away' as a social and political technology.
- Greater access to knowledge and dispersion of information empowers non-diplomats, particularly those policy actors and professionals working in internationalised policy domains.
- Diplomacy is 'de-institutionalised' from traditional institutions like MFAs and is increasingly regarded as a 'mode of behaviour'. Diplomatic roles in networks and partnerships are 'more related to knowledge capacity and capabilities and less to formal status' (Hocking and Melissen, 2016: 19).

Rather than seeing this pluralisation of diplomatic actors in negative terms as a 'withering away', a displacement or what has been termed elsewhere as the '*de*-professionalisation of diplomacy', these trends are better understood as '*trans*-professionalisation'. That is, 'as a productive development that reflects the expanded diplomatic space and the intensified pace of global interconnections and networks, and the new possibilities they unleash for practising diplomacy in different milieus' (Constantinou et al., 2016). Section 4 will pick up some of these themes concerning 'knowledge capacity and capabilities' where KNETs become tools for science diplomacy.

However, the point worth restating, not only is there digital disruption changing the face of diplomacy but there are also network processes and partnership innovations that also represent a major reconfiguration of state-centric diplomacy – one which has centred around MFAs, international civil servants, political leaders and diplomats – de-centred towards 'global policy' practices dispersed around a wider range of non-state actors. As individual entities, a particular TPPP in global health, or a specific TGN working on money laundering potentially become sites for diplomatic interactions. Transnational policy networks – in all their guises – harkens new fields of diplomatic engagement.

Conclusion

There are many varieties of transnational policy network. TGNs have greatest executive authority where government officials have a dual domestic and international function. Networks become tools for the extension of sovereignty where global problems are confronted by governmentally organised networks. What makes TGNs 'public' is that actors who compose them are formally designated power holders and rule makers who derive their authority from their official positions within their nation-state. Compared to TANs, which tend to be generated by 'bottom-up' strategic initiatives with solid foundations in civil society, TPPPs have greater official standing and public authority as they are usually initiated or convened by international organisations. TPRs are quite diverse ranging from regimes of self-regulatory norms and rules in a given issue area such as environmental management systems or certification of sustainable timber trade. TPRs also include the governance of global supply chains whereby firms at the consumer end of supply chains impose environmental quality standards on their suppliers, for instance, organic standards in agriculture. Or there are other corporate social responsibility initiatives where multinational corporations establish environmental standards for their global corporate network (like environmental safety standards in the chemical industry) (EEA, 2011: 100; also Cafaggi, 2019; Haufler, 2013).

In real world policy practice, these networks blur and overlap. However, the different power bases and organisation of transnational policy networks are observable. Towards the private end of the spectrum, TPPPs are defined by shared material interests and partnership principles in delivering public goods; TANs by their normative ambitions and advocacy orientation and TPRs with market standardisation and regulatory concerns. On the public end of the spectrum, TGNs are shaped by their political–legal character to be modes of trans-governmental public policy coordination. As discussed in the next section, KNETs are configured by their claims to epistemic authority.

By drawing attention to these distinctions, it is possible to better understand the ways in which power and policy authority are re-configured in global governance through policy networks. But no one network is alike. Where certain networks perpetuate power constellations, other types can help confront, contest and sometimes undermine entrenched power holders. TPPPs and TPRs may well privatise some aspects of policy design and delivery but TGNs act as a significant sovereignty-based counterweight while TANs at least uphold and advocate public values.

A comprehensive overview of all the institutions and networks functioning as part of global public-sector activity remains elusive. In the absence of firm definitions and a common lexicon, systematic mapping is not yet feasible. Instead, the messiness, fragmentation and ambiguity can be embraced. Our global public sector is highly differentiated. It does not have the neat symmetries seen at the nation-state level of governance where there are discernible government departments and agencies, recognised institutions for the enforcement of laws and regulations, or other official agencies for oversight and accountability, that are steered or directed by the core executive of government. Rather, the 'transnational state' – or the term preferred here, the global public sector – is a 'flexible networked cooperation of national state apparatuses and international organisations in an ongoing engagement with non-state actors, especially business' (Ougaard, 2018: 139). The kaleidoscopic variety of informal organisations, networks and partnerships means that it is contradictory to suggest that global policy is a rationally structured and 'integrated set of meaningful practices' (Puliot and Therien, 2017: 164). Instead, the disorderly patterns and practices that come with diverse funding flows, donor deliberations, policy innovations and personnel movements feed a multi-nucleated global public sector.

4 Global Policy Persuasion: From Evidence-Based Policy to Science Diplomacy

Experts rule! But experts are also ruled. In the global public sector, 'evidence-based policy' and 'science diplomacy' making is pronounced. Scholars and scientists – and many other experts found in think tanks, legal and consultancy firms or professional associations – sometimes compete and other times collaborate to shape institutional futures and policy trajectories in global governance. Experts co-author problem definition with government officials, are commissioned by international organisations and co-construct global policy institutions such as TPPPs. But they also move through their own knowledge networks (KNETs).

Public and private actors in transnational policy communities utilise (scientific) evidence in their daily work. As a result science diplomacy has become a 'both a driver and by-product' of the internationalisation of science (POST, 2018). Science diplomacy is usually linked to the foreign policy objectives of nation-states, but this phenomenon is increasingly linked to the efforts of some scientific communities to improve world affairs (Davis and Patman, 2015; Paár-Jákli, 2014). For instance, some agricultural scientists of CGIAR are engaged in 'rice diplomacy' (Okner, 2015). Ironically, our era of mounting global challenges is also an era of strong nationalist and populist sentiments (EL-CSID, 2019). Combined with the rise of 'alternative facts' and a 'post-truth' policy milieu, experts of all ilk face widespread scepticism (Woods, 2019). Nationalist-populist movements, and the political responses to them, can be a significant brake on the prospects and powers of epistocracies.

A key feature of many TANs, TGNs, TPPPs and TPRs is their foundation on (social) scientific knowledge and expertise. They incorporate expertise in some measure to define the cause-and-effect relations that create global problems, to guide policy action and to establish the mechanisms and social practices of cooperation and coordination between international organisations, their partners and other stakeholders in transnational policy communities. Expertise and evidence becomes an important source of legitimacy. And 'science' can play an important role as an 'epistemological arbiter' (Kouw and Petersen, 2018: 54). Yet, the use of 'science' and 'evidence' in global and regional institutions of governance is not an un-diluted public good. The activities of KNETs certainly promotes the power of experts and may also help entrench epistocracy in the making of global policy.

Knowledge Networks

'Wicked problems' like climate change, poverty and pandemic create uncertainty. In a world of countless cross-border problems, reassurance about policy uncertainties is sometimes found in 'science'. Over the past 30 years, an increasingly strong discourse emitting from governments and international institutions concerns the need to 'bridge research and policy' (Court and Young, 2006; Stone, 2013; Gilmore et al., 2018) and utilise K4D (Knowledge for Development) in the SDGs (see Hout, 2012: 408; Thompson, 2018, respectively). This knowledge utilisation discourse is symptomatic of the wider evidence-based policy movement that emerged in the political systems of the OECD countries towards the turn of the century (Head, 2013; Boswell, 2009). Recently, the lament of disconnect between evidence and decision-making, or research and policy development, has been reinvented in a new manifestation around 'science diplomacy'. Common to each manifestation is a desire for improved knowledge utilisation in governance in order to generate better, or better informed, policy processes and outcomes.

From the 1990s, the mantra that 'what matters is what works', entered the lexicon of government officials around the world. Evidence-based policy (EBP) proponents argue that rationality – understood as a utilitarian appraisal of policy problems and application of causal logics to achieve optimal socio-economic outcomes – should over-ride the value-laden dogma of ideological politics (Legrand and Stone, 2018). The superiority of 'rigorous' and 'objective' research is acclaimed (Solesbury, 2002: 95). This movement is based on a desire to be seen to be taking ideology and politics out of the policy process. Resort to 'experts' and their 'evidence' is one way to defuse – or de-politicise – policy making (Wood, 2019).

The externalisation of policy analysis and research is well recognised as having positive attributes in increasing the quality and variety of evidence, and the spread of innovation. Sometimes, the international dimensions are mentioned (Gluckman, 2016; Trondal, 2016), but EBP studies have tended to focus on domestic institutions and processes. A recent review acknowledges the gap, noting that more empirical inquiry is needed of 'supranational advisory units' (Craft and Halligan, 2017) especially concerning the role of expertise in international organisations (but see Littoz-Monnet, 2017; Knill and Bauer, 2018) and the role of professionals in transnational governance (Seabrooke and Henriksen, 2017).

Central to expert power in global policy processes are 'knowledge networks', or KNETs as shorthand. The value of networks to scientific advancement has long been noted with concepts like 'epistemic communities' (Haas, 2015) and the 'invisible college' (Wagner, 2009). Knowledge networks form around a shared scientific interest and are organised into a system of coordinated research to create and transfer knowledge. KNETs are characterised by practices such as regularised intellectual exchange, peer review and financing across national boundaries (Sending, 2019; Gross Stein et al., 2001: 6–7). KNETs are both 'scientific' and policy relevant. But KNETs take quite different shape. They differ on criteria of legal status, membership, degree of institutionalisation and issue focus. Regional networks have multiplied and are as diverse as the Baltic Science Network and the ASEAN Regional Knowledge Network on Forest Law Enforcement and Governance (ARKN-FLEG). There are also permanent global scientific entities like the Global Forum for Health Research, the Intergovernmental Panel on Climate Change (IPCC) or CGIAR which have long-term funding to employ secretariats and scientific officers.

There are many more temporary networks that coalesce around a specific project or funding stream. Philanthropic foundations have been financiers from the private sector, notably the Welcome Trust and the Gates Foundation in global health research. For decades, the European Commission has been supporting the research infrastructure of European KNETs, like the Baltic Science Network, through its Framework programmes and Horizon 2020. This support also reinforces the excellence of the Union's science base in order to make the Union's research and innovation system more competitive on a global scale. Prominent examples are the FET Flagships' of future and emerging technologies which are investments of billions of Euro in 10-year initiatives: 'European researchers unite forces to focus on solving an ambitious scientific and technological challenge, like understanding the Human Brain or developing the new materials of the future, such as Graphene' (H2020, 2019). Science and knowledge production are often presumed to naturally transcend borders and is thus is treated as an 'ideal vehicle' to promote 'political integration through social integration among experts and civil servants' (Sending, 2019: 384).

As instruments of for global policy making, KNETs are different from the TGNs, TANs or TPPPs discussed in the previous section in terms of their membership or composition. 'Most expert groups are based on some type of abstract knowledge that sets them apart from other actors' (Sending, 2019: 388). Individual or institutional inclusion in such networks is dependent upon either professional accreditation or official recognition of expertise such as developed through commitment to certain journals, conferences or other scientific gatherings that bestow scholarly and scientific credibility. Just as public-sector officials can only be members of a TGN, so too a participant in a KNET must be recognised as a qualified expert of some kind.

KNETs are essential for the international spread of research results, scientific practice and what is deemed international 'best practice' on matters as varied as green technologies, immunisation schemes, food security or of the uses of outer space. According to the UK Parliamentary Office for Science and Technology (POST), they are vehicles for 'getting science into policy'. This is because 'global challenges often require cross-disciplinary expertise from different countries' or for 'global negotiations' such as over climate change, where 'access to scientific evidence has been a vital component in steering consensus for joint action' (POST, 2018: 2).

KNETs do overlap into the network types outlined in the previous section, and they also flow through international organisations, inform treaty deliberations and inspire summits. For instance, the ASEAN knowledge network mentioned earlier – ARKN-FLEG – was created by an ASEAN Senior Officials meeting in 2008. Its main purposes are to provide evidence to support both ASEAN Ministers and their Senior Officials on Agriculture and Forestry 'in their decision-making and implementation processes by providing specific policy-oriented and -focused research and policy analysis' as well as by 'enhancing policy implementation capacity by mobilising resources and building partnerships to further strengthen FLEG implementation in ASEAN Member States; and ... at the regional and global levels' (DENR, 2019). In essence, ARKN-FLEG is both a KNET and a TGN.

Likewise, the IPCC is a high-profile example of a science intensive knowledge network. But as an 'inter-governmental panel' it is also 'political' (Ruffini, 2018: 74; Kouw and Petersen, 2018: 53). The Panel is also a TGN. The scientists appointed to it are appointed as representatives of their state. Even if they are normally based in a university or scientific laboratory and engage in scientific exchange through a variety of specialised tasks – they 'become aware that they are themselves doing politics' (Kouw and Petersen, 2018: 54; Gluckman et al., 2017). The IPCC can be regarded as an epistocratic arrangement for the review of climate trends and policy.

By no means unique, the IPCC is representative of one style of collaborative problem-solving processes through sharing of, and deliberating upon, accumulated knowledge and its consequences for policy makers. Other TPPPs – like the

Global Handwashing Partnership and the Gas Flaring initiative – are also very reliant upon, on the one hand, the medical evidence that has been built around the health benefits of sanitation and hygiene, and on the other, combinations of engineering, statistical and meteorological knowledge to contain flaring or the problems caused by it.

By focusing on KNETS, global policy making is seen to envelope different kinds of expert groups. Policy processes are not limited to those within the architecture of the state or based inside international organisations but extend to the knowledge networks flowing between them. In other words, the policies that are crafted around food security, or tackling anti-microbial resistance or promoting innovations in energy are linked to the theories, research programmes and expertise that supply these policies with objectives, targets, and other desired (usually measurable) outcomes. Accordingly, some KNETs and the forms of expertise they encompass can be viewed as an apparatus of rule, or what some consider to be a form of 'epistocracy' (Peters et al., 2018). That is, networks as vehicles for 'rule by knowers' (Klocksiem, 2019). The network form of organisation and knowledge mobilisation helps to centralise non-state actors – scientists and expert consultants – in the problematisation, management and monitoring of global issues. But what effects do they have?

De-politicising Global Policy Making

KNETs give their outputs – scientific reports, publications, analysis – and participants a patina of scientific objectivity and technocratic neutrality. Knowledge organisations also seek to validate their own conduct through scholarly standards and professional norms concerning peer review, rigorous methodologies and international rankings. However, sophisticated computer modelling, positive economic theories or scientific papers published in refereed professional journals create 'communication codes' that not only construct some knowledges as more persuasive or reliable but also work to exclude those who are not trained or educated in them. The 'communication codes' of science are not only expensive to reproduce but for the everyday citizen, these codes and processes of 'scientisation' (Zapp, 2018) are difficult to access. Mastering such codes usually require years of training. The distancing effect of scientific languages and scholarly practice are one important driver of depoliticisation in global policy processes.

There is now a substantial body of literature (see Woods, 2019) on the manner in which 'experts', and various forms of expertise, are argued to be central players in depoliticisation strategies in policy fields such as energy (Kuzemko, 2015) and the Kyoto climate change regime (Huggins, 2015) as well as policy design in general (Peters et al., 2018: 14). Depoliticisation also occurs when designing specific instruments like the targets of the SDGs; metrics such as these are described as 'calculative practices' of control (Ilcan and Phillips, 2008; Prince 2010). Transnational policy communities (attempt to) displace deliberation from politicians and the citizenry who are deemed to lack the capacity to make fully informed decisions due to the highly technical, complex or science-based character of the policy issue. 'Politics is framed as inefficient and bureaucratic and de/politicisation as a panacea for it: 'Politics is a pathogen; de-politicisation an antidote' (Beveridge and Naumann, 2014: 277). KNETs become instruments for depoliticisation.

Calls from governments or donor agencies or the international organisations for K4D and EBP have an effect of privileging experts. Policy deliberation is elevated to the epistocracy – rule by experts where (social) scientists are 'on top' – limiting wider participation and deliberation from non-experts. The power and authority of KNETs is vested in the epistemic credibility of the scientists and scholars equipped with their data and evidence, models and measures, theories and methodologies. However, rather than simply observing – monitoring and mapping problems and other phenomena – experts also enact and shape that reality. They are not simply advisory tools or wellsprings of information to be used by international organisations, governments or TPPPs as 'science on tap'. KNETs exercise professional agency in their own right as co-producers of governance (Jasanoff, 2004). Even so, KNETs remain heavily dependent on their relationships to centres of power qualifying considerably notions of epistocracy.

International Organisations and Transnational Policy Communities

International organisations have come to be important producers of policy knowledge in their own right (Littoz-Monnet, 2017). This is witnessed in the massive array of publications, reports and other forms of data produced by large and small international organisations alike. For example, adopting the moniker 'the Knowledge Bank', the World Bank has built substantial in-house expertise and professional capacity through its own large research department. Other units of the Bank undertake research, many members of staff hold doctorates (often in Law, Economics or 'development studies') and through adjunct professor positions work in colleges and universities.

UN agencies like the WHO or UNDP also have significant specialised expertise and employ staff of high academic or scientific standing. For example, at the Rio+20 Conference on Sustainable Development in 2012, the UN announced the instigation of the Secretary-Generals International Scientific

Advisory Board – but abolished it after a few years (Gluckman, 2018). Later the UN Environment Programme appointed a Chief Scientific Officer. In both cases, the intention was 'to ground multilateral decision-making in sound science' (Thompson, 2018).

Smaller specialised international organisations are also characterised by high reliance on scientific advice. The remit of the WTO covers science intensive fields such phytosanitary agreements and trade in advanced technologies or technology-based services whereby 'successful export, as well as import, depends on common technical standards and definitions' (Gluckman et al., 2017). Trade policy – which is not often thought to be deeply science based is in fact so – 'in the areas of food (Codex Alimentarius, *Codex*), animal health (World Animal Health Organisation, *OIE*), or plant diseases (International Plant Protection Convention, *IPCC*) . . . usually referred to as the 'Three Sisters', are of particular importance' in setting health and safety standards and creating an 'epistemic infrastructure' (Hornsby and Parshotam, 2018: 30–31).

Little attention is devoted to other small and relatively 'young' international organisations such as the Green Climate Fund established in 2010, or the Antarctic Treaty Secretariat created in 2003. By the very nature of their mandate, their operations rest upon marshalling scientific evidence. The International Commission for the Preservation of Atlantic Tunas (ICCAT), for instance, as well as several other international 'tuna commissions' are reliant on research carried out by marine scientists from national research institutes or universities based in member states. But ICCAT also convenes 'special research programmes' of its own as a mechanism to help focus, coordinate and complement those national research activities. 'Science underpins the management decisions made by ICCAT' declares this international organisation (ICCAT, 2019).

International organisations like the World Bank and the Food and Agricultural Organisation or species-specific bodies like ICATT are institutional nodal points for KNETs. By convening or resourcing TPPPs and KNETs, international organisations become an intermediary in the transfer of both knowledge and policy infrastructures. These pathways of policy transfer are not only between countries (as policy transfer is usually understood) but also circulate between global programmes and between other international organisations. If an internet visitor surfs the web-site of the Trust Funds and Partnerships unit of the World Bank they would quickly get the impression that this unit manages financial instruments for TPPPs 'focused on the provision of global public goods' (World Bank, 2019). But each policy domain requires scientific and social scientific knowledge and expertise to interpret the causes and consequences of pandemics, climate change and food insecurity. For instance, in global food policy, CGIAR conducted high-level research in its early years on breeding better staple food crops, expanding later to cover natural resource management, food production and ecoregions. Today, CGIAR research is organised into sixteen research programmes – ranging from gene banks, agroforestry or aquatic agricultural systems – across fifteen research centres including, inter alia, the International Potato Center and Bioversity International (CGIAR, 2019). In other words, the financial management of TPPPs becomes entwined with knowledge production.

Designing new TPPPs or sharing evidence and policy experience through KNETS and TGNs is an experimental process. This can have a recursive effect or what policy design scholars call 'non-design'. That is, 'interactions at the transnational level (including intergovernmental bargaining) are often about learning, especially in repetitive interactions' (Peters et al., 2018: 37). There were relatively few bodies like CGIAR in the 1990s. Yet, the 'CG model' – its network approach and 'epistemic infrastructure' – has been emulated in other policy sectors. This has happened through the funding priorities of donors and the convening role of key organisations like the UN and World Bank, which have propagated TPPPs, or the OECD which has facilitated TGN growth.

An organisational logic becomes established as a result of repeated cycles of learning around the shared professional experiences and epistemes. Networks are 'a privileged space in setting and deciphering the purpose of regulations' (Hornsby and Parshotam, 2018: 31). Instead of a one-way transmission of science and evidence into decision-making, transnational policy communities create an environment for social learning, in addition to epistemic learning, that helps create a sense of policy identity at an elite level within the organisational cultures of TPPPs, inside international organisations or through other transgovernmental venues.

Treating policy knowledge as the outcome of professional interaction, epistemic interpretation and bureaucratic socialisation helps undermine the frequently encountered ontological separation between the scholar and the policy practitioner, between knowledge and power. Instead, policy making and knowledge making are seen as mutually constituted or – in the current fashion of Policy Studies – 'co-constructed' through the practices of a transnational policy community (Tanczer et al., 2018). However, whether an epistocracy dominates the power relations of specific transnational policy communities is an empirical question to examine, and not a foregone conclusion.

Nevertheless, expert knowledge is mutually constituted with governance when transnational experts are consulted, contracted and co-author the creation of specific global policies or programmes. Their deliberations through TPPPs or

TGNs help fill the void of authority at global and regional levels where there are 'non-jurisdictional spaces' such as the oceans, the Antarctic or outer space (Gluckman et al., 2017; Witze, 2018). This co-construction is much more than simply blurred lines between public and private actors or between experts and political decision-makers. The term 'science diplomat' captures this fusion in global policy making.

The 'Science-Shaped Hole' in Global Policy Making

'Bridging Research and Policy' was a commonly heard statement in many EBP programmes during the 2000s. Today, this refrain has been reinvented in government initiatives seeking to 'bridge science and diplomacy' (Paár-Jákli, 2014). According to a former US Under Secretary for Economic Growth, Energy and the Environment, science is 'based on disciplines and values that transcend politics, languages, borders and cultures' (Hormats, 2012: 2). This universalist perspective of science as a benign global endeavour is a common refrain (Nedeva, 2013: 222). However, when science is linked to diplomacy, policy making is about epistemic persuasion.

In commonplace understanding, 'Science diplomacy' is *the use of scientific collaborations across nation-states* to address common problems and to build international partnerships (Fähnrich, 2017; Davis and Patman, 2015). Science diplomacy is 'documented primarily by those working in areas of global policy' as both a concept and a practice 'reflecting a period of increased global change' (Kaltofen and Acuto, 2018: 10). Although there are many definitions in play, one in particular has become frequently referenced (e.g. Smith, 2014; Flink and Schreiterer, 2010). The United Kingdom's Royal Society and the American Association for the Advancement of Science (AAAS) distinguish three modes of science diplomacy:

1. *science in diplomacy*, where scientific advice is used to inform foreign policy;
2. *diplomacy for science* whereby political resources are deployed to advance scientific research; and
3. *science for diplomacy*, whereby scientific cooperation is used to improve international relations. (Royal Society, 2010)

In policy practice, the three types blend together. This is evident in the case of the IPCC where diplomacy among nation-states (diplomacy for science) was essential to its creation as a TGN. Policy understandings of the changing nature of the global climate system has facilitated international agreements that are founded upon international scientific cooperation (science for diplomacy).

Scientific measurement and monitoring (science in diplomacy) is also crucial to the success of international climate agreements (Gluckman et al., 2017).

Tensions often emerge in trying to organise or promote science as a transnational endeavour for the (global) public good. There is a disjuncture between the scales of governance with 'the inherently global nature of the research fields and the localised, mostly national, research spaces' (Nedeva, 2013: 221). Research programmes are often grounded in national research institutes and universities, in national funding regimes and national systems for research evaluation, doctoral training and professional accreditation. The institutional logics of national research spaces can hinder the expansion and development of international scientific exchange and by extension, opportunities for science diplomacy despite the global nature of most research fields such as climate change, the SDGs, ozone depletion, biodiversity preservation, harvesting of the oceans, and cyber security (Tanczer et al., 2018). The institutional disjuncture is described as the 'science-shaped hole in global policy-making' by the president-elect of the International Science Council (Gluckman, 2018).

The understanding of diplomacy developed by the Royal Society and AAAS is concerned with improving *international cooperation*. Again, the key unit of analysis is the nation-state. States use scientific exchange and technical cooperation as a form of 'soft power' (Nye, 2005) to build trust and transparency in circumstances where other diplomatic ventures are thwarted. Nevertheless, the proliferation of transnational policy communities orbiting international organisations and criss-crossed by TGNs, TPRs and TPPPs do pose new questions about their transnational relations – indeed, their diplomatic roles and 'smart power' agency – in the global order.

The flowering of World Bank sponsored networks – such as CGIAR and the GDN mentioned earlier but also including many other bodies like the Global Forum for Health Research, the African Program for Onchocerciasis Control or the Global Partnership for Forest and Landscape Restoration – accelerate demand for research and technical expertise but present new political challenges. So too with UN agencies such as UNFIP's involvement in the Global Polio Eradication Initiative, or UNICEFs role in the Global Handwashing Partnership. These networks are not simply infrastructure to funnel development funds but present new domains of diplomacy (Kouw and Petersen, 2018).

Yet, the typology of the Royal Society and the American Academy reflects methodological nationalism. It addresses national mechanisms such as networks of science attachés based in embassies, science advisers inside MFAs, bilateral agreements and joint experimental facilities between countries as well as the roles of national academies. The typology needs refinement in order to take into account how transnational policy communities are addressing global challenges (Legrand and Stone, 2018):

1. Science *in* diplomacy as evidence *for* global policy actors. For example, the knowledge generated by epistemic communities such as the cetologists in the development of the International Whaling Commission (Haas, 2015: 17). Medical professionals inform health related TPPPs like 'Roll Back Malaria', The Stop TB Initiative and the partnership for Research and Training in Tropical Diseases.
2. Diplomacy *for* science to build trans-governmental capacity for science cooperation. CERN – Europe's high-energy physics laboratory near Geneva – is a well-known case (Höne and Kurbalija, 2018). Of special note is the European Commission's research agenda on Science and Cultural Diplomacy promoted through the Horizon 2020 grant scheme with funding for three separate KNETs on the topic (European Commission, 2014).
3. Science *for* diplomacy as transnational cooperation and understanding. Through global initiatives and KNETs (rather than inter-state cooperation), data and models as well as theories and concepts (such as GPGs) are put centre stage to cultivate 'international understanding'. The classic example is the Nobel Peace Prize–winning Pugwash Conference on Science and World Affairs with its tradition of 'dialogue across divides' to develop and support the use of scientific, evidence-based policy making around the risks associated for nuclear warfare and weapons of mass destruction.

One of the three H2020 KNETs funded by the European Commission is called EL-CSID – European Leadership in Cultural, Science and Innovation Policy (EL-CSID, 2019). The promotion of 'leadership' is clearly a political project. By the same token, use of a politically 'loaded' term like diplomacy inscribes science and knowledge creation as political rather than neutral projects of disinterested knowledge sharing.

The character of the science diplomat varies according to the policy problem or sector in which they are professionally engaged. We see practices of environmental diplomacy around the Critical Ecosystem Fund, or medical diplomacy around the Stop TB Initiative or Roll Back Malaria, and then again sustainable development diplomacy around the SDGs (Moomaw et al., 2017). CGIAR engages in scientific research on agriculture and aquaculture not only to assist country development plans and policy but also to inform relations with bodies like the Food and Agriculture Organization, the OECD and other international bodies involved in achieving the SDGs.

The goals stipulated in the SDGs are directly tied to global science exchange through the Technology Facilitation Mechanism (TFM). The TFM has three components: (1) a United Nations Interagency Task Team on Science, Technology and Innovation for the SDGs, including a 10-Member Group of representatives from civil society, the private sector and the scientific community; (2) a collaborative Multi-stakeholder Forum on Science, Technology and Innovation for the SDGs (STI Forum); and (3) an online platform as a gateway for information on existing STI initiatives, mechanisms and programmes. It is major effort of 'diplomacy for science' through 'multi-stakeholder collaboration and partnerships' (SDG Knowledge Platform, 2019). Yet, TFM has the power of persuasion only and its influence is ham-strung by the willingness (or not) of the nation-states that are party to the SDGs to listen and to respond.

Although the focus of this Elements is upon the domains and processes of global policy making, the pursuit of national interests in science diplomacy is not to be forgotten. The governments of major knowledge economies – China, Germany, South Korea, the UK and the USA – alongside the world's leading international organisations like the EU and the UN will remain central to controlling and coordinating global processes around science. Science for diplomacy can be used as a tool for economic warfare and sanctions. Take for instance the USA–China trade wars, with much of the focus now on banning US exports to Chinese technological firms or the plans by US lawmakers to tighten visas for Chinese students. American scientific superiority is utilised as a tool to achieve realist diplomatic ends. Science for diplomacy is geared around what is perceived to be the national interest. Science diplomacy through transnational policy communities can be undermined or thwarted, with potential consequences of hampering the delivery of GPGs for the rest of the world. Even so, when the Trump Administration announced US withdrawal from the Paris Climate Agreement more than 3,000 US cities, states, businesses and other groups declared their commitment to the Paris agreement. Their actions will put the USA within striking distance of the original commitment of 26 per cent reduction in greenhouse gases, by 2025 (Brown and Bloomberg, 2018). States and cities provide additional levels of governance for scientific networks to intersect.

However, the growth of transnational networks as well as bodies like the TFM pose new challenges for public-sector administration at all levels of governance. Policy officials in government agencies (beyond MFAs) are not necessarily adequately trained or equipped with the necessary technical skills to effectively engage with transnational policy communities. Building the transnational capacities of government agencies suggests bureaucratic reform as well as resourcing new directions in civil service training around TGN policy concerns. Training of this type is 'heavily underexplored from the point of view of professional education outside' of the diplomatic service (Kaltofen and Acuto, 2018: 13; Jones, 2019; Höne and Kurbalija, 2018).

National bureaucracies may need to see their public servants develop greater abilities in network management, sensitivity to inter-cultural difference on global policy issues; heightened bureaucratic competence to navigate not only the bureaucracies of international organisation but also global partnerships and international funding regimes; as well as enhanced professional knowledge of international benchmarking and 'soft law', and all of this in addition to mastering technical proficiency in substantive policy fields. So too, there is a growing need for training of doctoral candidates and young scientists to be engaged in good conduct for 'international professionalism in science' (Gluckman et al., 2017: Holford et al., 2017). Universities will increasingly look to recruit and train their own science diplomats given that the higher education sectors of many OECD countries are under fiscal and political pressure to demonstrate their 'impact' (Legrand and Stone, 2018).

Politicisation and Persuasion

The AAAS and Royal Society understanding of science in science diplomacy has been soundly criticised as 'benign and a-political' from perspectives where science is understood to be social, contextual, and contingent (Smith, 2014). More generally, science and technology studies (Jacobsen, 2007) or those from a constructivist perspective (Sending, 2019) identify further analytical deficiencies: the instrumentalisation of science; the linearity in thinking that the application of research and science leads in a one-way path to technological innovation or improved governance; and the inadequate consideration of power dynamics that can lead to the misuse, perversion or politicisation of scientific evidence. These criticisms have been levelled at national programmes but are equally valid for science-based TPPPs or for KNETs, which are also engaged in contests to define 'the truth'. That is, to develop a scientific foundation for a policy paradigm.

The phrase 'science diplomacy' has immense symbolic power: it signifies that those engaged in this practice are not only creators of scientific knowledge and theoretical models but that they are doubly useful for they are employed in what is depicted as a socially and political useful endeavour. In other words, 'the global communication processes by which scientific or other organized knowledge is being systematically applied to and inscribed by power politics' means that science diplomacy is inextricably bound with global governance (Der Derian, 1987: 202). Scientific discovery may well be ad hoc, experimental and curiosity-led, but science diplomacy is a strategic endeavour driven by political institutions.

Science diplomacy is thus a globalised form of evidence-based policy making. This purpose is reflected in the manner in which a number of governments, and the European Commission in particular, have become strong proponents of science diplomacy. For most governments, and in its original formulation, science diplomacy was seen as a means to promote national interests (Kaltofen and Acuto, 2018: 9). That is, designed to promote innovation and technological application for local industry. However, in the context of global challenges, the meaning and intent of science diplomacy has over the past decade widened to encompass normative aspirations rather than simply being a strategy to advance a country's national needs. For example, the 'EU approach' is complex. Rather than treating science diplomacy resulting *only* from national policies and science as a national jurisdiction, the funding programmes, the speeches of Directors General and the Commission's projection of 'Europe in the World' suggest there is a distinctive value-based approach to EU activity. The Commission is promoting science as a global public good and Europe as a 'global actor'.

When they are contracted as advisers for international organisations, or incorporated into transnational policy networks, scientists and scientific organisations also become enrolled into global governance. In this regard, science diplomacy can grow from bottom-up and unplanned practice. Science diplomacy evolves as a policy practice even if it is not 'named' as such. Scientific communities wield epistemic authority in their capacity to define the dimensions of policy problems and the policy routes of amelioration. As noted earlier, the IPCC provides the scientific understanding and consensus needed for effective international agreements on climate policy. By the same token, however, the IPCC is emblematic of the politicisation of scientific knowledge (Kouw and Petersen, 2018; Ruffini, 2018). Climate change science has been beset by accusations that climatologists have overstated or misrepresented the science. Climate science is emblematic of the deep degree to which there is scientific competition, alternative explanations and inconclusive data.

Not only is there a need to communicate the indeterminacy and risk associated with scientific inquiries for lay publics and policy communities, global policy making may also necessitate its own brand of science diplomat and knowledge networking. 'Knowledge brokers' (Gilmore et al., 2018) are needed to make science matter if it is to be relevant for global policy or international relations. The *communication* of policy relevant items of scientific research to political parties, bureaucrats and other decision-makers or regulators is an oft forgotten consideration in policy development but is essential to policy legitimation.

The proclivity to label global knowledge networking as science diplomacy has its own dangers. We may be witnessing an academic 'fad and fashion' (Davis and Patman, 2015), fuelled in some degree by European Commission funding into this topic. Quite suddenly, the IPCC was tagged as a science diplomat (see inter alia the November 2018 special issue of *Global Policy* and POST 2018). Now that IPCC is regarded as a science diplomat in the academic lexicon, soon other TGNs or TPPPs will be labelled in similar fashion. But there are limits to who and what can be called a diplomat or diplomatic practice.

Cultures of Fast Policy and Slow Science

'To speak truth to power' was originally voiced by the Quakers. For understanding the power of KNETs, knowledge in the form of scientific consensus presents an objective reality as a basis for policy reforms. Consensual knowledge takes the form of concrete knowledge of the physical world, objectively beholden by an epistemically privileged Cartesian observer (usually found in KNETs) who supposedly turns into a dispassionate adviser to the powerful (Stone, 2013). It is rationalist, technocratic approach to decision-making where the solutions to problems are presumed to be found by utilising the correct knowledge and evidence (Kouw and Petersen, 2018: 54). 'Truth speaks to power' as an 'art and craft of policy analysis' (Wildavsky, 1987; Head, 2013).

The effectiveness, and legitimacy, of science diplomacy within the public sphere rests in coalescing two different communities and two varying enterprises that connect 'research and the real world', 'knowledge and power', 'science and politics'. This is not necessarily an equal relationship. And too close proximity can call into question the integrity and legitimacy of the exercise (Cull, 2008: 36). These communities operate on 'two seemingly antagonistic modes of orientation and social interaction, one being the informal regime of academic peers, judgement and merits and the other formal organizations, authorities and hierarchies' (Flink and Schreiterer, 2010: 675). The challenge for global policy making is to 'respect the diversity of political interests without losing appreciation of ... science' (Kouw and Petersen, 2018: 54).

The incorporation of evidence and analysis, models and data, facts and figures into global policy making draws the scholar and scientist into policy. This is already a fraught issue with vastly differing positions on the role of the university in society and economy and notions of 'responsible scholarship' (Jones, 2019; Sending, 2019). Science and scholarship on the one hand, and policy and politics on the other, are often assumed to be separated by identifiable social, legal and organisational boundaries where the two operate in different ecologies. Echoing the view of the US Science Counsellor outlined earlier:

> the appeal of science in public policy rests upon the assumption that scientific conclusions are value-free and thus independent of the use to which they are put … Boundary-defining strategies demarcate science from non-science, facts from values. However, the balancing-act between usability and scientific credibility also points to the arbitrariness of these boundaries and the problems associated with idealistic images of scientific purity. (Lövbrand, 2007: 41)

There are more boundaries. As discussed in Section 2, one boundary is between the national and the international. Another fluid boundary is in determining who or what practices are inside or outside a network of organisations. In the case of many TPPPs and TGNs, evidence does not come from 'outside' the network but very often is generated within it.

Science Counsellors are nationally organised in MFAs. They have a vested interest to delimit the use of the term 'science diplomacy and its practice to their professional undertakings and relationships. For instance, during a 2018 meeting in Brussels of EU member state Science Counsellors with the European Commission, one group raised 'the danger of labelling everything as diplomacy' (Anonymous, 2018). There are also different priorities and norms between MFAs and knowledge organisations: MFAs are focused on science *diplomacy* whereas national Academies of Science and universities are driven by scientific *cooperation and research excellence* criteria.

MFAs pursue the national interest, and this primary pursuit may mean on occasion curtailing the international interactions of their national scientific communities. Some states with scientifically superior knowledge economies may seek to reassert their authority through various forms of control over their national scientific and scholarly communities working either at home or abroad. For example, the Chinese government's direct support for, and control over, Chinese student groups in countries such as the USA, UK, Canada and Australia has attracted media and political attention. Visa approvals (or denial) are an obvious tool of control regarding international collaboration and conferences.

Science diplomacy reveals other contradictions as a mode of EBP. Policy making often works in a hot-house environment requiring rapid responses to impending public issues. By contrast, knowledge creation is usually a slow measured process of inquiry that cannot always be fast-tracked to meet the latest crisis. Just as Lindblom's (1959) seminal article 'The Science of "Muddling Through"' argued that policy making is a series of incremental steps characterised by trial and error, so too, science is a creative and experimental process composed of dead-ends and near-misses. Rather than a rational-linear process of a cascading epistemic consensus through knowledge accumulation, science is very often contested (Reiss, 2019). And frequently, its uses are political (Sending, 2019). Consequently, many scientists and researchers are reluctant to associate with political activity. And the notion they are, or could be, 'diplomats' has generated a backlash in some quarters.

The concept of 'science diplomacy' is not owned by scientific communities or KNETs. Instead, science diplomacy is a policy concept and a construct driven by governments and the European Commission alike. The reluctance of academics to become involved in diplomacy was recognised at the Brussels Science Counsellors meeting because: 'It sounds as if there is an alternative (ulterior) motive' (Anon, 2018). The last thing that many scientists want to be is a branch of government. For example, a Spanish émigré scientist wrote an inspired piece in the prestigious journal *Nature* that the new Spanish government strategy for science diplomacy was no more than a cover-up for extensive funding cut-backs of research institutions that forced a brain-drain out of the country. Re-labelled as 'brain circulation', the 'science diaspora is being recruited as "partners" not only to enhance Spain's presence in key countries but also allow the Spanish Government take credit for the science done and funded abroad, and claim it is "Made in Spain"' (Moro-Martin, 2017).

Among some scientific communities there is concern the policy push for science diplomacy could influence the daily work of scientists. That is, the policy discourse of science diplomacy is regarded as intrusion into 'normal' processes of knowledge exchange and scientific collaboration. Among other scholars, there is concern that external audiences will become suspicious of the EU through its science diplomacy activities and they caution that this type of activity not be seen as a new mode of neo-colonialism. For instance, for many African states, their engagement with science diplomacy is 'as "consumers" rather than "producers" of knowledge and expertise' (Hornsby and Parshotam, 2018: 30; Šehović, 2017). Another long-standing concern, first voiced in a speech of US President Eisenhower, is the possible negative impact of an expanding military-industrial complex on the conduct of research in universities (Smart, 2016).

Given the concerns and criticisms emerging from the scholarly world about science diplomacy as an evidence-based approach to global policy development, there is a proclivity among them to avoid or find alternatives for the phrase 'diplomacy'. For example, the more politically neutral language of 'civic science' (Okner, 2015) and 'open science' (Anon, 2018) or to represent science as GPG provision (Thompson, 2018: 45). In the case of CGIAR, all fifteen of its research centres signed on to an Open Access and Data Management Policy in 2013. This step was presented as both a commitment to GPG delivery as well as a form of public accountability. Also in support of open science, the 'All European Academies' – an association of learned academies – advocates that publicly funded research be accessible 'on open access platforms and thereby realise "science as a global public good"' (ALLEA, 2018). If not the language of GPGs or 'open science', there is often a strong narrative preference for the apolitical terms of 'partnership' or scientific 'collaboration' or 'exchange'. These types of professional norms and cultures of (social) science represent self-imposed restraints on the emergence of epistocracy in transnational policy communities.

Conclusion: Power and Persuasion among Partners

Earlier, it was stated that science diplomacy is a globalised form of evidence-based policy making. But science diplomacy is much more than a one-way process of pushing evidence into policy deliberation. The information gathering, technical monitoring and sustained research into matters such as the SDG targets, levels of CO_2 in the atmosphere, the growing problems of 'space junk' and so forth that are pursued through the expert and policy deliberations of KNETs, TPPPs and TGNs develops an administrative infrastructure. The imbrication of science in policy means that expert communities are co-constructing the architectures of the global public sector. 'Bridging research and policy' or 'science diplomacy' becomes a form of policy coordination. But the growing diversity of transnational administrative bodies like the TPC for the SDGS, or the IPPC on climate issues, or the European Space Agency networking with other space agencies around the risks associated with space junk (Witze, 2018) – also creates fragmentation, unclear boundaries between public and private domains of policy making, and opaque lines of both authority and accountability.

The policy discourse of EBP – including science diplomacy – has tended to overlook the choices that are made about what to research and how to undertake that research (Head, 2013; Wood, 2019). Furthermore, particular types of evidence are often favoured in policy making. Evidence that is quantifiable and amenable to 'measurement' or 'setting targets' or which is more malleable for policy purposes privileges one type of evidence over others. That is, models and metrics – such as the SDGs and the Basel 4 standard on capital reserves for banks, or ISO guidelines on how countries quantify their greenhouse gas emissions – become devices that structure individual and organisational behaviours as well as that of nation-states. The choice of evidence is value-laden and political in itself. Finally, de-politicising dynamics to dampen ideology or politics in global policy processes by appeals to the evidence or 'science' (Thompson, 2018) are potentially undemocratic when – or if – an epistocracy and 'rule by knowers' comes to dominate power relations among a transnational policy community. Whether global governance comes to be dominated by democracy, epistocracy or other ruling regimes is currently in the making.

5 Navigating Global Policy Processes

Making policy is as central to transnational domains as it is to national and local domains. However, global policy is constituted differently. Decision-making authority and policy implementation is not grounded solely in the authority of sovereign nation-states or inter-governmental organisations acting on their behalf. Already, international public administration is established in the formal setting of the EU (Bauer et al., 2018) and other international organisations. But this phenomenon is paralleled by transnational administrations serving TPPPs and informal international organisations. With a multitude of policy initiatives and various forms of GPG financing, a global public sector is slowly taking shape. Transnational policy communities in fields as diverse as global health, global energy policy or regional migration policy as well as operating across the management of global commons like the oceans and outer space provide 'differentiation' to the shape of the global public sector. In this milieu, epistocracies – with their power grounded in their professional and scientific knowledge – may also become embedded.

As this volume in the Elements series has sought to convey, a central feature of the global policy is its network character. Towards this end, the discussion has distinguished between five different types of transnational policy network: KNETs, TANs, TGNs, TPPPs and TPRs. In order to be effective, local and national government officials often need to respond to transnational policy problems in collaboration with their counterparts in foreign governments; with international civil servants in international organisations and the executives of global public–private partnerships, as well as with expert partners in research communities and scientific associations. Networks are often the mechanism for collaboration. By focusing on network relations, rather than formal power holders in centres of power like the UN system, analytical focus is shifted to informal processes and practices across different interstices of governance (Pouliot and Therien, 2018). This focus on the informal also shines a light on the powers of expert groups that are seeking to define the causes of global policy problems and establish agendas on how best to ameliorate them.

GPGs is one key concept around which the practice of global policy revolves. Transnational policy networks can be regarded not only as delivery mechanisms of GPGs but also as having the properties of 'intermediate' GPGs because they contribute towards the provision of final public goods (Kaul, 2019: 266). One indispensable task that they perform is that of monitoring and surveillance. On the global level, state failure is a given 'due to the absence of a global sovereign' to enforce compliance in the provision of public goods. As a consequence, the nature of power changes as well. Rather than reliance on state sanctions and coercive powers to ensure policy delivery, transnational policy networks and informal international organisations represent 'smart power' strategies enabling states to achieve desired policy outcomes (Boonen et al., 2018).

As this is a short volume, it is not possible to convey the vast diversity of global policy initiatives and 'GPG policy spaces' (Kaul, 2019) that have emerged. A major challenge for policy scholars concerns how to best capture in data and map the infrastructure for the administration of global policies. To date, analysis has been limited to overviews of specific policy sectors – migration, global health or global environmental policy. While incredibly valuable studies in their own right, these analyses create an issue focus, rather than addressing the policy making architectures of environment, migration, health and all other policy fields in the aggregate (inter alia Biermann, 2009; Faist, 2012; Šehović, 2017). That is, the interconnections between these policy fields that may exist in terms of common organisational logics and administrative protocols or similar network mechanisms and funding instruments. While the policy design of global governance has been ad hoc and experimental, nevertheless a global public-sector architecture – weak though it may be in terms of institutional consolidation and formal authority – has taken root and is growing.

Next steps in understanding global policy are to build a greater analytic appreciation of transnational bureaucracies of TPPPs and TPRs and the international public administrations inside international organisations. In Policy Studies this requires an analytical sensibility geared towards 'methodological transnationalism'. In the main, the independent variable in the study of IR is the state (as both black box and actor). By contrast, a focus on 'global policy processes' transfers the status of the state from that of an independent to a dependent variable. Relegating the state to the status of just one socio-political jurisdiction of policy making and administration amongst others, allows us to recognise authoritative decision-making and public goods provision across the multiple transnational policy communities of the global public sector (Stone and Ladi, 2015). Returning to the idea of administrative sovereignty, TPPPs maintain 'a reasonable measure of autonomy, credibility, and reliability over time' (Muth, 2019: 62) to be considered transnational administrations.

Nation-state sovereignty is challenged by this new public-sector architecture. But sovereignty persists and remains important in curtailing the powers of TPPPs through controls on funding or by governments simply choosing to ignore the advocacy of TANs. Similarly, governments can control scientific communities and other types of 'expert' through their powers to appoint, to fund and to accredit or patronise. To mix metaphors, there is a constant tug of war between politicians, civic activists, community leaders and government officials to keep scientific and professional communities 'on tap' rather than 'on top'. Moreover, national governments and local authorities are the prime actors in the implementation of global and regional policies. The manner in which street-level bureaucrats at these levels interpret and negotiate policy can also create a series of brakes to the imposition of global policies. Counter-intuitively, sovereignty is also bolstered in some circumstances. TGNs strengthen the capacities of states to confront global problems through cross-national bureaucratic cooperation.

There will be increased pressure upon national administrations and local authorities to prepare their civil servants for a greater degree of policy communication and coordination with counterparts in administrations in other countries, in international entities – both formal (like UN agencies) and informal (like the BRICs and G20) – and in transnational policy communities. This entails allocations of resources to participate in such networks as well as a re-thinking the nature of civil service training. Not all bureaucracies and government agencies have the internal capacity to absorb the scientific evidence and policy experience generated by transnational policy communities. Nor do all states have the human or financial resources to participate on an equal footing in global policy processes. Power differentials will persist and become preponderant.

An enduring concern for the policy scholar is the connection between policy and democracy or in the context here, between global policy and transnational democracy. For many people whose lives are based in 'everyday communities' and focused on parochial concerns, transnational democracy may have little meaning. The appeal of populism and nationalism can have greater traction within societies and lead to pressures for de-globalisation – processes to curtail or diminish interdependence and integration between nation-states. De-globalisation could include restricting the powers of transnational policy communities. In many ways, transnational policy communities are venues for the rule of the knowers. Even so, their 'rule' (limited as it is) and scientific evidence is contested as is their legitimacy on other normative grounds of justice, fairness and equity. Indeed, much of this contestation comes from within the academy:

> experts need to be kept in check, not given more power. Scientific conclusions – theories, concepts, facts – are enormously useful for individual and political decision making, but only if they are regarded as that: tools for thinking (and not as commands for action). (Reiss, 2019: 191)

An interesting question for future examination is the extent to which knowers and others involved in decision-making act in ways that maximises the epistemic quality of transnational policy communities. That is, that the paradigm around which the transnational policy community revolves is based on sound and valid knowledge. This opens up, first, the question of the extent to which relevant actors are motived to maximise epistemic quality and to act on the basis of their best knowledge, as opposed to the manner in which they may seek to maximise their professional or organisational interests (Holst, 2012). Again, an application of the 'bureau-shaping' model (Dunleavy, 2014) could shed much light here.

The prospects for global policy debate and deliberation that incorporates multiple voices is not bleak. Transnational policy networks do offer some prospect for civic participation as 'an inclusive space of negotiation' and as venues for 'new diplomats' (Kouw and Petersen, 2018: 55). Focusing on the interdependence of different interests wrought by globalisation suggests that if stakeholders are included, then networks offer a supplement to territorially organised representative democracy: First, stakeholder input represent a means to increase the quality of policy outputs – improved 'governability'. Second, networks contribute to the empowerment of groups, enhancing prospects for reasoned deliberations and enlivening new forms of accountability. Finally, networks are also mechanisms for groups, movements, citizens to launch critique, opposition and dissent (see Sorenson and Torfing, 2005). Indeed, particular types of network such as TANs have power to advocate and advance normative policy agendas.

Nevertheless, the operations of transnational policy networks also cast significant and problematic questions of transparency, representation and accountability. A critical perspective warns that networks constitute a serious threat to liberal democracy for a number of reasons. First, they undermine polyarchy by creating clubs possessing political influence with restricted and unevenly distributed access. The limited transparency of networks reduces capacity of the public to be aware and informed so as to control, regulate and hold accountability the actions of network elites. The delegation of decision-making competences and processes to networks – many of which can be of private constitution – undermines the capacity of elected representatives to control networks and their actions.

Networks blur the demarcation between public and private further hampering openness. The opaque private face of networks can hide how particularistic interests rise to the fore or how networks provide fertile environment for the creation of alliances that co-opt representatives from (global) civil society thereby undermining the autonomy of institutions of civil society. Finally, transnational networks in particular, can undermine the link between nation-state and the demos (Sorenson and Torfing, 2005: 214–15).

Without the development of strong and binding principles of transparency and representation to rein in transnational policy networks, a gradual de-democratisation and disenfranchisement of those not enveloped within networks, or who are excluded from networks due to their lack of professional, political or epistemic credentials, could lead to an erosion of democratic accountabilities. Indeed, the global public sector may well come to be managed by epistocracies – potentially with anti-egalitarian tendencies – in the absence of a global demos. Today, and for the foreseeable future, the rights and responsibilities of citizenship are more often than not, brought to a halt at nation-state borders. As a consequence, the global public sector is managed primarily by powerful 'stakeholders', policy elites and expert interests. These issues echo President Eisenhower in his 1961 speech critical of the military-industrial complex and who also cautioned that 'in holding scientific research and discovery in respect, as we should, we must also be alert to the equal and opposite danger that public policy could itself become the captive of a scientific-technological elite'.

For CEU, the Central European University

The fate of CEU – forced out of Hungary by the legislative onslaught of a self-declared 'illiberal government' – is a stark reminder of the enduring power of the nation-state. The nationalist-populist policies of the Órban government have prevailed despite sustained political pressure from the European Commission on its recalcitrant member state to revise the higher education legislation of 2017. Commonly known as Lex CEU, the fate of this university in exile has revealed the limitations of aspirations favouring the universality of science and scholarship, the democratic foundations of the European project of regional integration and the prospects for global policy collaboration.

Abbreviations

AAAS	American Association for the Advancement of Science
ALLEA	All European Academies
APEC	Asia-Pacific Economic Cooperation
APN	Anglosphere policy networks
ARKN-FLEG	ASEAN Regional Knowledge Network on Forest Law Enforcement and Governance
ASEAN	Association of Southeast Asian Nations
BMGF	Bill and Melinda Gates Foundation
BRICS	Brazil, Russia, India, China, South Africa
DAC	Development Advisory Committee (of the OECD)
DG	Directorate General (of the European Commission)
DGF	Development Grant Facility (of the World Bank)
EBP	evidence-based policy
ECOSOC	United Nations Economic and Social Council
EEA	European Environment Agency
EEAS	European External Action Service
EITI	Extractive Industry Transparency Initiative
EL-CSID	European Leadership in Cultural, Science and Innovation Diplomacy
EU	European Union
FATF	Financial Action Task Force
FCTC	Framework Convention for Tobacco Control
FSC	Forest Stewardship Council
G20	Group of Twenty Nations
GAIN	Global Alliance for Improved Nutrition
GAL	global administrative law
GAVI	Global Alliance for Vaccines and Immunisation
GCDP	Global Commission on Drug Policy
GGFR	global gas flaring reduction
GPG	global public good
GPP	global (public) policy
GPPi	Global Public Policy institute
GPPN	Global Public Policy Network
GPPP	global public–private partnerships
HIV/AIDS	human immunodeficiency virus/acquired immune deficiency syndrome

IAIS	International Association of Insurance Supervisors
ICCAT	International Commission for the Conservation of Atlantic Tunas
IIGO	informal intergovernmental organisation
ILO	International Labour Organization
IMF	International Monetary Fund
IMO	International Maritime Organisation
INGO	international non-governmental organisation
INGSA	International Network for Government Science Advice
IO	international organisation
IPCC	Intergovernmental Panel on Climate Change
IR	International Relations
ISEAL	International Social and Environmental Accreditation and Labelling Alliance
ISO	International Organization for Standardization
K4D	Knowledge for Development
KNET	knowledge network
MDTF	multi-donor trust fund
MFA	Ministry of Foreign Affairs
MNC	multi-national corporation
MSF	Médecins Sans Frontières/Doctors without Borders
NGO	non-governmental organisation
NPM	new public management
OECD	Organisation for Economic Co-operation and Development
PPP	public–private partnership
RTD	Research Training Directorate (of the European Commission)
SDG	Sustainable Development Goals
STI	science, technology and innovation
TAN	Transnational Advocacy Coalition
TGN	trans-governmental networks
TPR	transnational private regulation
UK	United Kingdom
UN	United Nations
UNDP	United Nations Development Programme
UNEP	United Nations Environmental Programme
UNICEF	United Nations International Children's Emergency Fund
UNF	United Nations Foundation
US/USA	United States of America
V4	Visegrad Four
WEF	World Economic Forum

WFP	World Food Programme
WG	working group
WHO	World Health Organization
WMO	World Meteorological Organization
WTO	World Trade Organization

References

Agerskov, A. H. (2005, May) 'Global public goods and development – a guide for policy makers', in *Seminar Number 6: World Bank Seminar Series at Kobe and Hiroshima Universities. Global Development Challenges Facing Humanity.* Washington, DC: World Bank. http://siteresources.worldbank.org /EXTABOUTUS/Resources/PublicGoods.pdf

Alimi, D. (2015) '"Going global": Policy entrepreneurship of the Global Commission on Drug Policy', *Public Administration, 93*(4):874–89.

ALLEA (2018) 'All European academies response to Plan S', December, www .allea.org/wp-content/uploads/2018/12/ALLEA_Response_PlanS.pdf

Andia, T., & Chorev, N. (2017) 'Making knowledge legitimate: transnational advocacy networks' campaigns against tobacco, infant formula and pharmaceuticals', *Global Networks, 17*(2):255–80.

Andonova, L. B. (2017) *Governance Entrepreneurs: International Organizations and the Rise of Global Public–Private Partnerships.* Cambridge: Cambridge University Press.

Anonymous (2018) Notes on Science Counsellors Meeting, November, Brussels.

Babb, S. (2013) 'The Washington Consensus as transnational policy paradigm: Its origins, trajectory and likely successor', *Review of International Political Economy, 20*(2):268–97.

Bäckstrand, K., and Kylsäter, M. (2014) 'Old wine in new bottles? The legitimation and delegitimation of UN public–private partnerships for sustainable development from the Johannesburg Summit to the Rio+ 20 Summit', *Globalizations, 11*(3):331–47.

Bäckstrand, K., Campe, S., Chan, S., Mert, A., and Schäferhoff, M. (2012) 'Transnational public–private partnerships', in Bierman, F., and Pattberg, P. (Eds) *Global Environmental Governance Reconsidered.* Cambridge, MA: MIT Press.

Bauer, M. W., Ege, J., and Schomaker, R. (2018) 'The challenge of administrative internationalization: Taking stock and looking ahead', *International Journal of Public Administration, 42*(11):904–17.

Bauman, E., and Miller, S. D. (2012) *Comprehensive Literature Review of Global Public Policy: Creating a Framework for Understanding Global Refugee Policy.* Working Paper Series Number 87, Oxford: Refugee Studies Centre.

Beisheim, M., and Ellersiek, A. (2017). 'Partnerships for the 2030 Agenda for Sustainable Development: transformative inclusive and accountable?' Stiftung Wissenschaft und Politik, Berlin, SWP Research Paper 2017/14.

Beisheim, M., and Simon, N. (2018) 'Multistakeholder partnerships for the SDGs: actors' views on UN metagovernance', *Global Governance*, *24*(4):497–515.

Beveridge, R., and Naumann, M. (2014) 'Global norms, local contestation: Privatisation and de/politicisation in Berlin', *Policy & Politics 42*(2):275–91.

Biermann, F. (2009) *Managers of Global Change: The Influence of International Environmental Bureaucracies*. Cambridge, MA: MIT Press.

Biermann, F., and Siebenhüner, B. (2013). 'Problem solving by international bureaucracies', in Reinalda, B. (Ed) *Routledge Handbook of International Organization*. London: Routledge.

Birdsall, N., and Diofasi, A. (2015) *Global Public Goods for Development: How Much and What For*. Washington, DC: Center for Global Development.

Birkland, T. A. (2016) *An Introduction to the Policy Process: Theories, Concepts and Models of Public Policy Making*, 4th edn. New York: Routledge.

Bodansky, D. (2012) 'What's in a concept? Global public goods, international law, and legitimacy', *European Journal of International Law*, *23*(3):651–68.

Boonen, C., Brando, N., Cogolati, S., Hagen, R., Vanstappen, N., and Wouters, J. (2018) 'Governing as commons or as global public goods: An analysis of normative discourses', Leuven Centre for Global Governance Studies, Institute for International Law, Working Paper 203, https://ssrn.com/abstract=3271711

Boswell, C. (2009) *The Political Uses of Expert Knowledge: Immigration Policy and Social Research*. Cambridge: Cambridge University Press.

Broome, A., and Seabrooke, L. (2015) 'Shaping policy curves: Cognitive authority in transnational capacity building', *Public Administration 93*(4):956–72.

Brown, J., and Bloomberg, M. (2018) 'Even without the Trump administration, the US is upholding the Paris Agreement', *Climate Home News*, www.climatechangenews.com/2018/09/12/even-without-trump-administration-us-upholding-paris-agreement/

Budd, L., Bell, M., and Brown, T. (2009) 'Of plagues, planes and politics: Controlling the global spread of infectious diseases by air', *Political Geography 28*(7):426–35.

Burchardt, M., Patterson, A. S., and Rasmussen, L. M. (2013) 'The politics and anti-politics of social movements: Religion and HIV/AIDS in Africa', *Canadian Journal of African Studies 47*(2):171–85.

Büthe, T., and Mattli, W. (2013) *The New Global Rulers: The Privatization of Regulation in the World Economy*. Princeton, NJ: Princeton University Press.

Cafaggi, F. (2019) 'Compliance in transnational regulation', in Stone, D., and Moloney, K. (Eds) *The Oxford Handbook of Global Policy and Transnational Administration*. Oxford: Oxford University Press.

Carbonnier, G. (Ed) (2012) *International Development Policy: Aid, Emerging Economies and Global Policies*. Berlin: Springer.

Castells, M. (2011) *The Rise of the Network Society*. Hoboken, NJ: John Wiley.

Cerny, P. G. (2017) 'The limits of global governance: Transnational neopluralism in a complex world', in *Partnerships in International Policy-Making*. London: Palgrave Macmillan.

CGIAR (2019) CGIAR Research Programs, www.cgiar.org/our-strategy/cgiar-research-programs/

Clifton, J., and Díaz-Fuentes, D. (2011) 'From 'club of the rich' to 'globalisation à la carte'? Evaluating reform at the OECD', *Global Policy*, *2*(3):300–11.

Constantinou, C. M., Cornago, N., and McConnell, F. (2016) 'Transprofessional diplomacy', *Brill Research Perspectives in Diplomacy and Foreign Policy*, *1*(4):1–66.

Cooper, T. L., and Yoder, D. E. (1999) 'The meaning and significance of citizenship in a transnational world: Implications for public administration', *Administrative Theory & Praxis*, *21*(2):195–204.

Corry, O. (2010) 'What is a (global) polity?' *Review of International Studies*, *36*(S1):157–80.

Court, J., and Young, J. (2006) 'Bridging research and policy in international development: An analytical and practical framework', *Development in Practice*, *16*(1):85–90.

Craft, J., and Halligan, J. (2017) 'Assessing 30 years of Westminster policy advisory system experience', *Policy Sciences*, 50(1):47–62.

Crump, L., and Downie, C. (2018) 'The G20 chair and the case of the Global Economic Steering Committee', *Global Society*, *32*(1):23–46.

Cull, N. J. (2008) 'Public diplomacy: Taxonomies and histories', *Annals of the American Academy of Political and Social Science*, *616*(1):31–54.

DAC Network on Evaluation (2014) 'Evaluation in global and regional multi-donor trust funds and partnership programs: How to proceed', Development Assistance Committee of the Organisation for Economic cooperation and Development, 16th Meeting, 12–13 February.

Davis, L. S., and Patman, R. G. (Eds) (2015) *Science Diplomacy: New Day or False Dawn*. New York: World Scientific.

Dawes, S. S., and Gharawi, M. A. (2018) 'Transnational public sector knowledge networks: A comparative study of contextual distances', *Government Information Quarterly, 35*(2):184–94.

Dawes, S. S., Gharawi, M. A., and Burke, G. B. (2012) 'Transnational public sector knowledge networks: knowledge and information sharing in a multi-dimensional context', *Government Information Quarterly, 29*:S112–20.

Deacon, B. (2007) *Global Social Policy and Governance*. Thousand Oaks, CA: Sage.

De Búrca, G., Keohane, R. O., and Sabel, C. (2014) 'Global experimentalist governance', *British Journal of Political Science, 44*(3):477–86.

De Oliveira, O. P. (2017) *International Policy Diffusion and Participatory Budgeting: Ambassadors of Participation, International Institutions and Transnational Networks*. New York: Springer.

Department of Environment and Natural Resources (2019) ASEAN Regional Knowledge Network on Forest Law Enforcement and Governance (ARKN-FLEG), DENR, Government of Philippines, http://intl.denr.gov.ph/index.php/asean-menu/asean-groups/asean-networks/article/2

Der Derian, J. (1987) *On Diplomacy*. Oxford: Basil Blackwell.

Drache, D. (2001) 'The return of the public domain after the triumph of markets: Revisiting the most basic of fundamentals', in Drache, D. (Ed) *The Market or the Public Domain*. London: Routledge.

Dryzek, J. S. (2006). *Deliberative Global Politics: Discourse and Democracy in a Divided World*. Cambridge: Polity.

Dunleavy, P. (2014) *Democracy, Bureaucracy and Public Choice: Economic Approaches in Political Science*. New York: Routledge.

Dye, T. (1984) *Understanding Public Policy*. Englewood Cliffs, NJ: Prentice Hall.

Eaton, S., and Porter, T. (2008) 'Globalization, autonomy and global institutions: accounting for accounting', in Pauly, L. W., and Coleman, W. D. (Eds) *Global Ordering: Institutions and Autonomy in a Changing World*. Vancouver: UBC Press.

Eisenhower, D. (1960) *Public Papers of the Presidents, Dwight D. Eisenhower, 1960*, 1035–40, https://avalon.law.yale.edu/20th_century/eisenhower001.asp

EL-CSID (2018) Steering Committee Meeting, 12 November.

EL-CSID (2019) *Final Report: European Leadership in Cultural, Science and Innovation Policy*, Brussels, February, www.el-csid.eu/

Elliott, L. (2012) 'ASEAN and environmental governance: Strategies of regionalism in Southeast Asia', *Global Environmental Politics, 12*(3):38–57.

Eriksen, S. S., and Sending, O. J. (2013) 'There is no global public: The idea of the public and the legitimation of governance', *International Theory*, 5(2):213–37.

European Commission (2014) 'Communication from the Commission to the European Parliament, the Council, the European Economic and Social committee and the Committee of the Regions: Report on the implementation of the strategy for international cooperation in research and innovation', COM (2014) 567 final, Brussels, 11 September.

European Environment Agency (201) *Global Governance: The Rise of Non-state Actors*. EEA Technical Report 4. Luxembourg: Publications Office of the European Union.

Evans, M. (2019) 'International policy transfer', in Stone, D., and Moloney, K. (Eds) *The Oxford Handbook of Global Policy and Transnational Administration*. Oxford: Oxford University Press.

Evans, J. W., and Davies, R. (Eds) (2014) *Too Global to Fail: The World Bank at the Intersection of National and Global Public Policy in 2025*. Washington, DC: World Bank.

Fähnrich, B. (2017) 'Science diplomacy: Investigating the perspective of scholars on politics–science collaboration in international affairs', *Public Understanding of Science*, 26(6):688–703.

Faist, T. (2012) 'Toward a transnational methodology', *Revue européenne des migrations internationales*, 28(1):51–70.

Falkner, R. (Ed) (2016) *The Handbook of Global Climate and Environment Policy*. Hoboken, NJ: John Wiley.

Fanoulis, E., and Musliu, V. (2018) 'Sovereignty a-venir: towards a normative understanding of sovereignty', *Global Society*, 32(1):70–87.

Farazmand, A., and Pinkowski, J. (Eds) (2007) *Handbook of Globalization, Governance, and Public Administration*. Boca Raton, FL: Taylor and Francis.

Flink, T., and Schreiterer, U. (2010) ''Science diplomacy at the intersection of S&T policies and foreign affairs: Towards a typology of national approaches', *Science and Public Policy*, 37(9):665–6.

Fraser, N. (2013) *Fortunes of Feminism: From State Managed Capitalism to Neoliberal Crisis*. Brooklyn, NY: Verso.

GAVI (2019) 'GAVI's mission', www.gavi.org/about/mission/

Gergen, K. J. (2014) 'From mirroring to world-making: Research as future forming', *Journal for the Theory of Social Behaviour*, 45(3):287–310.

Geuijen, K., Moore, M., Cederquist, A., Ronning, R., and van Twist, M. (2017) 'Creating public value in global wicked problems', *Public Management Review*, 19(5):621–39.

Gilmore, E. A., Risi, L. H., Tennant, E., and Buhaug, H. (2018) 'Bridging research and policy on climate change and conflict', *Current Climate Change Reports*, 4(4):313–19.

Global Policy Forum (2014) *Beyond the 'Partnerships' Approach: Corporate Accountability Post-2015*. GPF Briefing 2. New York: Global Policy Forum.

Gluckman, P. (2016) 'Science advice to governments: An emerging dimension of science diplomacy', *Science and Diplomacy*, 5(2), www.sciencediplomacy.org /article/2016/science-advice-governments

Gluckman, P. D. (2018) 'How to fill the science shaped hole in global policy-making', *INGSA Blog*, www.ingsa.org/ingsa-news/article-how-to-fill-the-science-shaped-hole-in-global-policymaking-peter-gluckman/

Gluckman, P. D., Turekian, V., Grimes, R. W., and Kishi, T. (2017) 'Science diplomacy: A pragmatic perspective from the inside', *Science and Diplomacy*, 6(4).

Green, A. (Ed) (2016) *Handbook of Global Education Policy*. Hoboken, NJ: John Wiley.

Gross Stein, J., Stren, R., Fitzgibbon, J., and MacLean, M. (2001) *Networks of Knowledge: Collaborative Innovation in International Learning*. Toronto: University of Toronto Press.

H2020 (2019) Future and Emerging Technologies, Horizon 2020. https://ec .europa.eu/programmes/horizon2020/en/h2020-section/future-and-emerging-technologies Accessed October 4th 2019.

Haas, P. M. (2015) *Epistemic Communities, Constructivism, and International Environmental Politics*. New York: Routledge.

Hadjiisky, M., Pal, L. A., and Walker, C. (Eds) (2017) *Public Policy Transfer: Micro-dynamics and Macro-effects*. London: Edward Elgar.

Harrow, J., and Jung, T. (2019) 'Providing foundations: Philanthropy, global policy and administration', in Stone, D., and Moloney, K. (Eds) *The Oxford Handbook of Global Policy and Transnational Administration*. Oxford: Oxford University Press.

Haufler, V. (2013) *A Public Role for the Private Sector: Industry Self-Regulation in a Global Economy*. Washington, DC: Brookings Institution Press.

Head, B. W. (2013) 'Evidence-based policymaking – speaking truth to power?' *Australian Journal of Public Administration*, 72(4):397–403.

Heasman, M., and Lang, T. (2015) *Food Wars: The Global Battle for Mouths, Minds and Markets*. New York: Routledge.

Heemskerk, E. M., Fennema, M., and Carroll, W. K. (2016) 'The global corporate elite after the financial crisis: Evidence from the transnational network of interlocking directorates', *Global Networks*, 16(1):68–88.

Held, D., Dunleavy, P., and Nag, E. (2010) 'Editorial statement', *Global Policy*, *1*(1), https://doi.org/10.1111/j.1758-5899.2009.00017.x

Held, D., and Koenig-Archibugi, M. (2004) 'Introduction: special issue on global governance and public accountability', *Government and Opposition*, *39*(2):125–31.

Hocking, B., and Melissen, J. (2016) 'Diplomacy and digital disruption', in Hofmeister, W., and Melissen, J. (Eds) *Rethinking International Institutions: Diplomacy and Impact on Emerging World Order*. Singapore: Konrad Adenauer Stiftung and Netherlands Institute of International Relations.

Hodge, G., and Greve, C. (2018) 'Contemporary public–private partnership: Towards a global research agenda', *Financial Accountability and Management*, *34*(1):3–16.

Hoffmann, A. M. (2019) *Regional Governance and Policy-Making in South America*. Cham, Switzerland: Palgrave Macmillan.

Holford, M., and Nichols, R. W. (2017) 'The challenge of building science diplomacy capabilities for early career academic investigators', *Science and Diplomacy*, *6*(4).

Holst, C. (2012) 'Epistocracy: conceptual clarifications', mimeo, University of Oslo.

Höne, K. E., and Kurbalija, J. (2018) 'Accelerating basic science in an inter-governmental framework: Learning from CERN's science diplomacy', *Global Policy*, *9*:67–72.

Horizon 2020 (2019) 'Future and emerging technologies', https://ec.europa.eu/programmes/horizon2020/node/94

Hormats, R. D. (2012) 'Science diplomacy and twenty-first century statecraft', *Science and Diplomacy*, *1*(1), www.sciencediplomacy.org/perspective/2012/science-diplomacy-and-twenty-first-century-statecraft

Hornsby, D. J., and Parshotam, A. (2018) 'Science diplomacy, epistemic communities, and practice in sub-Saharan Africa', *Global Policy*, *9*:29–34.

Hout, W. (2012) 'The anti-politics of development: Donor agencies and the political economy of governance', *Third World Quarterly*, *33*(3):405–22.

Hoxtell, W. (2017) *Multi Stakeholder Partnerships and the 2030 Agenda: Challenges and Options for Oversight at the United Nations*. Berlin: GPPi.

Huggins, A. (2015) 'The desirability of depoliticization: Compliance in the international climate regime', *Transnational Environmental Law* *4*(1):101–24.

Ilcan, S., and Phillips, L. (2008) 'Governing through global networks knowledge mobilities and participatory development', *Current Sociology*, *56*(5):711–34.

International Commission for the Conservation of Atlantic Tunas (2019) 'Home', www.iccat.int/en/index.asp

Independent Evaluation Program (IEG) (2007) *Sourcebook for Evaluating Global and Regional Partnership Programs Indicative Principles and Standards*. Washington, DC: World Bank.

Islam, S., and Susskind, L. (2012) *Water Diplomacy: A Negotiated Approach to Managing Complex Water Networks*. New York: Routledge.

Jacobson, N. (2007) 'Social epistemology: Theory for the "fourth wave" of knowledge transfer and exchange research', *Science Communication*, *29*:116–27.

Jasanoff, S. (Ed) (2004) *States of Knowledge: The Co-production of Science and the Social Order*. London: Routledge.

Jeffrey, A. (2018) 'Limited epistocracy and political inclusion', *Episteme*, *15*(4):412–32.

Jenks, B. (2012) 'The United Nations and global public goods', in Carbonnier, G. (Ed) *International Development Policy: Aid, Emerging Economies and Global Policies*. New York: Springer.

Jones, S. (2019) 'This bridge feels like a tightrope: For critical scholars who engage in policy research', *American Behavioral Scientist*, *63*(3):404–420.

Jordana, J. (2017) 'Transgovernmental networks as regulatory intermediaries: Horizontal collaboration and the realities of soft power', *Annals of the American Academy of Political and Social Science*, *670*(1):245–62.

Kaan, C., and Liese, A. (2011) 'Public private partnerships in global food governance: Business engagement and legitimacy in the global fight against hunger and malnutrition', *Agriculture and Human Values*, *28*(3):385–99.

Kaltofen, C., and Acuto, M. (2018) 'Science diplomacy: introduction to a boundary problem'. *Global Policy*, *9*:8–14.

Kamruzzaman, P. (2013) 'Civil society or "comprador class", participation or parroting?', *Progress in Development Studies*, *13*(1):31–49.

Kaul, I. (2019) 'A global public good perspective', in Stone, D., and Moloney, K. (Eds) *The Oxford Handbook of Global Policy and Transnational Administration*. Oxford: Oxford University Press.

Kaul, I., and Conceição, P. (Eds) (2006) *The New Public Finance: Responding to Global Challenges*. Oxford: Oxford University Press.

Kauppinen, I. (2015) 'Towards a theory of transnational academic capitalism', *British Journal of Sociology of Education*, *36*(2):336–53.

Keck, M., and Sikkink, K. (1998) *Activists beyond Borders: Advocacy Networks in International Politics*. Ithaca, NY: Cornell University Press.

Keohane, R. O., and Nye, J. S. (1974) 'Transgovernmental relations and international organizations', *World Politics*, *27*(1):39–62.

Kerr, P., and Wiseman, G. (Eds) (2013) *Diplomacy in a Globalizing World: Theories and Practices*. New York: Oxford University Press.

Khoo, M. S. (2019) 'Law-Space Nexus, Global Governance and Global Administrative Law', in Stone, D., and Moloney, K. (Eds) *The Oxford Handbook of Global Policy and Transnational Administration*. Oxford: Oxford University Press.

Kingah, S., Schmidt, V. A., and Yong, W. (2015) 'Setting the scene: The European Union's engagement with transnational policy networks', *Contemporary Politics, 21*:231–44.

Kingsbury, B., Krisch, N., and Stewart, R. B. (2005) 'The emergence of global administrative law', *Law and Contemporary Problems 68*(3–4):15–61.

Klassen, T. R., Cepiku, D., and Lah, T. J. (Eds) (2016) *The Routledge Handbook of Global Public Policy and Administration*. New York: Taylor and Francis.

Kleinschmidt, J., and Strandsbjerg, J. (2010) 'After critical geopolitics: why international relation theory needs even more social theory', paper presented at the Millennium Conference, October.

Klocksiem, J. (2019) 'Epistocracy is a wolf in wolf's clothing', *Journal of Ethics, 23*(1):19–36.

Knill, C., and Bauer, M. W. (Eds) (2018) *Governance by International Public Administrations: Bureaucratic Influence and Global Public Policies*. New York: Routledge.

Kouw, M., and Petersen, A. (2018) 'Diplomacy in action: Latourian politics and the Intergovernmental Panel on Climate Change', *Science and Technology Studies, 31*(1):52–68.

Krasner, S. (1999) *Sovereignty: Organized Hypocrisy*. Princeton, NJ: Princeton University Press.

Kuzemko, C. (2015) 'Energy depoliticisation in the UK: Destroying political capacity'. *British Journal of Politics and International Relations, 18* (1):107–24.

Lee, K. (2001) 'The global dimensions of cholera', *Global Change and Human Health, 2*(1):6–17.

Legrand, T. (2015) 'Transgovernmental policy networks in the Anglosphere', *Public Administration, 93*(4):973–91.

Legrand, T. (2019) 'Sovereignty renewed: transgovernmental policy networks and the global-local dilemma', in Stone, D., and Moloney, K. (Eds) *The Oxford Handbook of Global Policy and Transnational Administration*. Oxford: Oxford University Press.

Legrand, T., and Stone, D. (2018) 'Science diplomacy and transnational governance impact', *British Politics, 13*(3):392–408.

Lindblom, C. E. (1959) 'The science of muddling through'. *Public Administration Review, 19*(2):79–88.

Littoz-Monnet, A. (Ed) (2017) *The Politics of Expertise in International Organizations: How International Bureaucracies Produce and Mobilize Knowledge.* New York: Routledge.

López de San Román, A., and Schunz, S. (2018) 'Understanding European Union science diplomacy', *Journal of Common Market Studies, 56*(2):247–66.

Lövbrand, E. (2007) 'Pure science or policy involvement? Ambiguous boundary-work for Swedish carbon cycle science', *Environmental Science and Policy, 10*(1):39–47, http://sciencepolicy.colorado.edu/admin/publica tion_files/resource-2487-2007.04.pdf

Machacek, K. M. (2018) 'Global public–private partnerships and the new constitutionalism of the refugee regime', *Global Constitutionalism, 7*(2):204–35.

Mamudu, H., Cairney, P., and Studlar, D. (2015) 'Global public policy: Does the new venue for transnational tobacco control challenge the old way of doing things?' *Public Administration, 93*(4):856–73.

Martens, J. (2007) *Multistakeholder Partnerships – Future Models of Multilateralism?* Berlin: Friedrich-Ebert-Stiftung, http://citeseerx .ist.psu.edu/viewdoc/download?doi=10.1.1.583.8582&rep=rep1&type=pdf

Merriam-Webster (2019) 'Definition of public policy', www.merriam-webster.com/dictionary/public%20policy

Meseguer, C. (2005) 'Policy learning, policy diffusion, and the making of a new order'. *Annals of the American Academy of Political and Social Science, 598* (1):67–82.

Milhorance, C. (2018) *New Geographies of Global Policy-Making: South-South Networks and Rural Development Strategies.* New York: Routledge.

Mitzen, J. (2005) 'Reading Habermas in anarchy: multilateral diplomacy and global public spheres', *American Political Science Review, 99*(3):401–17.

Moloney, K., and Stone, D. (2019) 'Beyond the state: Global policy and transnational administration', *International Review of Public Policy, 1*(1):104–18.

Moomaw, W. R., Bhandary, R. R., Kuhl, L., and Verkooijen, P. (2017) 'Sustainable development diplomacy: Diagnostics for the negotiation and implementation of sustainable development', *Global Policy, 8*(1):73–81.

Moro-Martin, A. (2017) 'How dare you call us science diplomats', *Nature, 543*:289.

Murphy-Gregory, H., and Kellow, A. (2016) 'Forum shopping and global governance', in Hofmeister, W., and Melissen, J. (Eds) *Rethinking*

International Institutions: Diplomacy and Impact on Emerging World Order. Singapore: Konrad Adenauer Stiftung and Netherlands Institute of International Relations.

Muth, K. T. (2019) 'The potential and limits of administrative sovereignty', in Stone, D., and Moloney, K. (Eds) *The Oxford Handbook of Global Policy and Transnational Administration.* Oxford: Oxford University Press.

Nagel, S. S. (1991) *Global Policy Studies: International Interaction toward Improving Public Policy.* London: Palgrave Macmillan.

Nedeva, M. (2013) 'Between the global and the national: Organising European science', *Research Policy*, 42(1):220–30.

Newman, E., and Ravndal, E. (2019) 'The International Civil Service', in Stone, D., and Moloney, K. (Eds) *Oxford Handbook of Global Policy and Transnational Administration.* Oxford: Oxford University Press.

Nishimuzu, M. (2000) 'TB control – why it makes development sense', www.stoptb.org/events/meetings/amsterdam_conference/nishimizuspeech.asp

Nye, J., Jr. (2005) *Soft Power: The Means to Success in World Politics.* New York: Public Affairs.

OECD (2019) 'Trans-governmental networks', www.oecd.org/gov/regulatory-policy/irc7.htm

Okner, T. (2015) 'The role of research institutions in civic science and sustainable development diplomacy', *CGSpace: A Repository of Agricultural Research Outputs*, https://cgspace.cgiar.org/handle/10568/65200

Operations Evaluation Department (OED) (2002) *The World Bank's Approach to Global Programs: An Independent Evaluation Phase 1 Report.* Washington, DC: World Bank.

Orenstein, M. A. (2005) 'The new pension reform as global policy', *Global Social Policy*, 5(2):175–202.

Ougaard, M. (2018) 'The transnational state and the infrastructure push', *New Political Economy*, 23(1):128–44.

Ougaard, M., and Higgott, R. (2002) *Towards a Global Polity.* New York: Routledge.

Paár-Jákli, G. (2014) *Networked Governance and Transatlantic Relations: Building Bridges Through Science Diplomacy.* New York: Routledge.

Pal, L. (2019) 'Standard setting and international peer review: The OECD as a transnational policy actor', in Stone, D., and Moloney, K. (Eds) *The Oxford Handbook of Global Policy and Transnational Administration.* Oxford: Oxford University Press.

Pamment, J. (2013) *New Public Diplomacy in the 21st Century: A Comparative Study of Policy and Practice.* Abingdon, UK: Routledge.

Parliamentary Office of Science and Technology (2018) 'Science diplomacy', *POSTNOTE*, no. 568, February.

Patriota, G., Castellano, A., and Wright, M. (2013) 'Coordinating knowledge transfer: global managers as higher-level intermediaries', *Journal of World Business*, *48*(4):515–26.

Pattberg, P., and Widerberg, O. (2016) 'Transnational multistakeholder partnerships for sustainable development: Conditions for success', *Ambio*, *45*(1):42–51.

Peck, J., and Theodore, N. (2015) *Fast Policy*. Minneapolis: University of Minnesota Press.

Peters, B. G., Capano, G., Howlett, M., Mukherjee, I., Chou, M. H., and Ravinet, P. (2018) *Designing for Policy Effectiveness: Defining and Understanding a Concept*. Cambridge: Cambridge University Press.

Pouliot, V., and Thérien, J. P. (2018) 'Global governance in practice', *Global Policy*, *9*(2):163–72.

Prince, R. (2010) 'Globalizing the creative industries concept: Travelling policy and transnational policy communities', *Journal of Arts Management, Law, and Society*, *40*(2):119–39.

Reinicke, W. (1998) *Global Public Policy: Governing without Government*, Washington, DC: Brookings Institution Press.

Reinicke, W. H., and Deng, F., with Witte, J. M., Benner, T., and Whitaker, B. (2000) *Critical Choices: The United Nations, Networks, and the Future of Global Governance*. Ottawa, ON: IDRC.

Reiss, J. (2019) 'Expertise, agreement, and the nature of social scientific facts; or, Against epistocracy', *Social Epistemology*, 33(2):183–92.

Ronit, K. (Ed) (2007) *Global Public Policy: Business and the Countervailing Powers of Civil Society*. New York: Routledge.

Ronit, K. (2018) *Global Business Associations*. New York: Routledge.

Royal Society (2010) *New Frontiers in Science Diplomacy: Navigating the Changing Balance of Power*. London: Royal Society.

Ruffini, P. B. (2018) 'The Intergovernmental Panel on Climate Change and the science-diplomacy nexus', *Global Policy*, 9:73–7.

Ruggie, J. G. (2004) 'Reconstituting the global public domain – issues, actors, and practices', *European Journal of International Relations*, *10*(4):499–531.

Ruggie, J. G. (2015) 'Life in the global public domain: Response to commentaries on the UN Guiding Principles and the Proposed Treaty on Business and Human Rights', 23 January, https://ssrn.com/abstract=2554726

Sassen, S. (2016) *Global Networks, Linked Cities*. New York: Routledge.

Schäferhoff, M., Campe, S., and Kaan, C. (2009) 'Transnational public–private partnerships in international relations: Making sense of concepts, research frameworks, and results', *International Studies Review, 11*(3):451–74.

Schneiker, A., and Joachim, J. (2018) 'Revisiting global governance in multistakeholder initiatives: Club governance based on ideational prealignments', *Global Society, 32*(1):2–22.

Schomaker, R. M. (2017) 'Public-private governance regimes in the global sphere', *Public Organization Review, 17*(1):121–38.

SDG Knowledge Platform (2019) 'Technology facilitation mechanism', https://sustainabledevelopment.un.org/tfm

Seabrooke, L., and Henriksen, L. F. (Eds) (2017) *Professional Networks in Transnational Governance*. Cambridge: Cambridge University Press.

Šehović, A. B. (2017) *Coordinating Global Health Policy Responses: From HIV/AIDS to Ebola and Beyond*. Berlin: Springer.

Sending, O. J. (2016) 'The transformation of international publicness', in Hofmeister, W., and Melissen, J. (Eds) *Rethinking International Institutions: Diplomacy and Impact on Emerging World Order*. Singapore: Konrad Adenauer Stiftung and Netherlands Institute of International Relations.

Sending, O. J. (2019) 'Knowledge networks, scientific communities, and evidence-informed policy', in Stone, D., and Moloney, K. (Eds) *The Oxford Handbook of Global Policy and Transnational Administration*. Oxford: Oxford University Press.

Severino, J.-M., and Ray, O. (2009) 'The end of ODA: Death and rebirth of a global public policy', 25 March, https://ssrn.com/abstract=1392460

Skogstad, G. (Ed) (2011) *Policy Paradigms, Transnationalism and Domestic Politics*. Toronto, ON: University of Toronto Press.

Slaughter, A.-M. (2004) *A New World Order*. Princeton, NJ: Princeton University Press.

Slaughter, A.-M. (2017) 'Global government networks, global information agencies, and disaggregated democracy', in *Public Governance in the Age of Globalization*. New York: Routledge.

Slaughter, S. (2015) 'Building G20 outreach: The role of transnational policy networks in sustaining effective and legitimate summitry', *Global Summitry, 1*(2):171–86.

Smart, B. (2016) 'Military-industrial complexities, university research and neoliberal economy'. *Journal of Sociology, 52*(3):455–81.

Smith, Frank L., III (2014) 'Advancing science diplomacy: Indonesia and the US Naval Medical Research Unit', *Social Studies of Science, 44*(6):825–47.

Solesbury, W. (2002) 'The ascendancy of evidence', *Planning Theory and Practice, 3*(1):90–96.

Sorenson, E., and Torfing, J. (2005) 'Network governance and post liberal democracy', *Administrative Theory and Praxis, 27*(2):197–237.

Soroos, M. (1986) *Beyond Sovereignty: The Challenge of Global Sovereignty.* Columbia, SC: University of South Carolina Press.

Standke, K. H. (2006) 'Science and technology in global cooperation: The case of the United Nations and UNESCO', *Science and Public Policy, 33*(9):627–46.

Stibbe, D. T., Reid, S., and Gilbet, J. (2018) *Maximising the Impact of Partnerships for the SDGs.* New York: The Partnering Initiative and UN DESA.

Stone, D. (2013) *Knowledge Actors and Transnational Governance: The Private-Public Policy Nexus in the Global Agora.* New York: Palgrave Macmillan.

Stone, D., and Ladi, S. (2015) 'Global public policy and transnational administration', *Public Administration, 93*(3):839–55.

Stone, D., and Moloney. K. (Eds) (2019) *The Oxford Handbook of Global Policy and Transnational Administration.* Oxford: Oxford University Press.

Strandsbjerg, J. (2010) *Territory, Globalization and International Relations: The Cartographic Reality of Space.* Basingstoke: Palgrave Macmillan.

Stubbs, P. (2013) 'Flex actors and philanthropy in (post-) conflict arenas: Soros' Open Society Foundations in the post-Yugoslav space'. *Politička misao: časopis za politologiju, 50*(5):114–38.

Sun, Y. (2017) 'Transnational public-private partnerships as learning facilitators: Global governance of mercury', *Global Environmental Politics, 17*(2):21–44.

Susskind, L. E., and Ali, S. H. (2014) *Environmental Diplomacy: Negotiating More Effective Global Agreements.* Oxford: Oxford University Press.

Tanczer, L. M., Brass, I., and Carr, M. (2018) 'CSIRTs and global cybersecurity: how technical experts support science diplomacy', *Global Policy, 9*:60–6.

Thompson, H. E. (2018) 'Science Diplomacy within Sustainable Development: A SIDS Perspective', *Global Policy, 9*(S3):45–47.

Thurner, P. W., and Binder, M. (2009) 'European Union transgovernmental networks: The emergence of a new political space beyond the nation-state?', *European Journal of Political Research, 48*(1):80–106.

Trondal, J. (2016) 'Advances to the study of international public administration', *Journal of European Public Policy, 23*(7):1097–108.

True, J. (2003) 'Mainstreaming gender in global public policy', *International Feminist Journal of Politics, 5*(3), 368–96.

Tsingou, E. (2015) 'Club governance and the making of global financial rules', *Review of International Political Economy 22*(2):225–56.

Turner, B. S. (1993) 'Outline of a theory of human rights', in Turner, B. S. (Ed) *Citizenship and Social Theory.* London: Sage.

United Nations Foundation (2002) 'Understanding public private partnerships', www.globalproblems-globalsolutions-files.org/unf_website/PDF/under stand_public_private_partner.pdf

Vabulas, F. (2019) 'The administration of informal intergovernmental organisations', in Stone, D., and Moloney, K. (Eds) *Oxford Handbook of Global Policy and Transnational Administration.* Oxford: Oxford University Press.

Verger, A., Altinyelken, H. K., and Novelli, M. (Eds) (2012) *Global Education Policy and International Development: New Agendas, Issues and Policies.* London and New York: Bloomsbury.

Vogelpohl, A. (2019) 'Global expertise, local convincing power: Management consultants and preserving the entrepreneurial city', *Urban Studies 56*(1):97–114.

Volkmer, I. (2019) 'The transnationalization of public spheres and global policy', in Stone, D., and Moloney, K. (Eds) *The Oxford Handbook of Global Policy and Transnational Administration.* Oxford: Oxford University Press.

Wagner, C. S. (2009) *The New Invisible College: Science for Development.* Washington, DC: Brookings Institution Press.

Weller, P., and Xu, Y.-C. (2019) 'Heads of international organizations: Politicians, diplomats, managers', in Stone, D., and Moloney, K. (Eds) *Oxford Handbook of Global Policy and Transnational Administration.* Oxford: Oxford University Press.

Wildavsky, A. (1987) *Speaking Truth to Power: The Art and Science of Policy Analysis.* New Brunswick, NJ: Transaction.

Witze, A. (2018) 'The quest to conquer Earth's space junk problem', *Nature 561*: 24–26.

Wood, M. (2019) *HyperActive Governance: How Governments Manage the Politics of Expertise.* Cambridge: Cambridge University Press.

World Bank (2019) 'What are financial intermediary funds', http://fiftrustee .worldbank.org/Pages/FIFSOverview.aspx

Yeates, N. (Ed) (2008) *Understanding Global Social Policy.* London: Policy Press.

Yeates, N. (Ed) (2014) *Understanding Global Social Policy.* London: Policy Press.

Yu, Y., Chan, A. P., Chen, C., and Darko, A. (2017) 'Critical risk factors of transnational public–private partnership projects: Literature review', *Journal of Infrastructure Systems*, *24*(1).

Zapp, M. (2018) 'The scientization of the world polity: International organizations and the production of scientific knowledge, 1950–2015', *International Sociology*, *33*(1):3–26.

Acknowledgements

This Element was written whilst working at the University of Canberra and the University of Warwick. This study has received funding from the European Union's Horizon 2020 research and innovation programme under grant agreement 693799 as part of the 'European Leadership in Cultural, Science and Innovation Diplomacy' (EL-CSID) project. The discussion and analysis within this Element do not necessarily reflect the opinions of the EU.

Cambridge Elements ☰

Public Policy

M. Ramesh
National University of Singapore (NUS)

M. Ramesh is UNESCO Chair on Social Policy Design at the Lee Kuan Yew School of Public Policy, NUS. His research focuses on governance and social policy in East and Southeast Asia, in addition to public policy institutions and processes. He has published extensively in reputed international journals. He is Co-editor of Policy and Society and Policy Design and Practice.

Michael Howlett
Simon Fraser University, British Colombia

Michael Howlett is Burnaby Mountain Professor and Canada Research Chair (Tier 1) in the Department of Political Science, Simon Fraser University. He specialises in public policy analysis, and resource and environmental policy. He is currently editor-in-chief of *Policy Sciences* and co-editor of the *Journal of Comparative Policy Analysis; Policy and Society* and *Policy Design and Practice.*

Xun WU
Hong Kong University of Science and Technology

Xun WU is Professor and Head of the Division of Public Policy at the Hong Kong University of Science and Technology. He is a policy scientist whose research interests include policy innovations, water resource management and health policy reform. He has been involved extensively in consultancy and executive education, his work involving consultations for the World Bank and UNEP.

Judith Clifton
University of Cantabria

Judith Clifton is Professor of Economics at the University of Cantabria, Spain. She has published in leading policy journals and is editor-in-chief of the *Journal of Economic Policy Reform.* Most recently, her research enquires how emerging technologies can transform public administration, a forward-looking cutting-edge project which received €3.5 million funding from the Horizon2020 programme.

Eduardo Araral
National University of Singapore (NUS)

Eduardo Araral is widely published in various journals and books and has presented in forty conferences. He is currently Co-Director of the Institute of Water Policy at the Lee Kuan Yew School of Public Policy, NUS and is a member of the editorial board of *Journal of Public Administration Research and Theory* and the board of the Public Management Research Association.

About the series

Elements in Public Policy is a concise and authoritative collection of assessments of the state of the art and future research directions in public policy research, as well as substantive new research on key topics. Edited by leading scholars in the field, the series is an ideal medium for reflecting on and advancing the understanding of critical issues in the public sphere. Collectively, it provides a forum for broad and diverse coverage of all major topics in the field while integrating different disciplinary and methodological approaches.

Cambridge Elements $\equiv$

Public Policy

Elements in the series

Designing for Policy Effectiveness: Defining and Understanding a Concept
B. Guy Peters, Giliberto Capano, Michael Howlett, Ishani Mukherjee, Meng-Hsuan Chou and Pauline Ravient

Making Policy in a Complex World
Paul Cairney, Tanya Heikkila and Matthew Wood

Pragmatism and the Origins of the Policy Sciences: Rediscovering Lasswell and the Chicago School
William N. Dunn

The Protective State
Christopher Ansell

How Ideas and Institutions Shape the Politics of Public Policy
Daniel Béland

Policy Entrepreneurs and Dynamic Change
Michael Mintrom

Making Global Policy
Diane Stone

A full series listing is available at: www.cambridge.org/EPPO